Life is Not a
Destination

Books by Ben Mukkala:

"Thoughts Along the Way - Secrets of a Happy Life" Selected Columns

"Life is Not a Destination"

Audio Version, "Life is Not a Destination"

"Touring Guide, Big Bay & Huron Mountains"

"Come On Along, Tales and Trails of the North Woods"

"Copper, Timber, Iron and Heart, Stories from Michigan's Upper Peninsula"

Life is Not a Destination

by

Ben Mukkala

Still Waters Publishing
Marquette, Michigan
© 2005

Life is Not a Destination

Copyright 2005
Ben Mukkala

All photography in this book is the work of the author
unless indicated otherwise.

Published by Still Waters Publishing, 2005

Printing Coordinated by Globe Printing, Ishpeming, Michigan
www.globeprinting.net

Limited First Edition • 1,500 copies • March 2005
Second Edition • 1000 copies • November 2007

ISBN   0-9709971-4-0
ISBN   978-0-9709971-4-0

"You may covet your wealth and thank God for your health but life's stories will last you - forever."

"Life is Not a Destination"

It's what you do along the way.

Life is Not a Destination

Dedication

"... The purpose of life is to *matter* – to count, to stand for something, to have it make some difference that we have lived at all."

This book is respectfully dedicated to

You,

The Reader

If these pages inform you, if you enjoy them, if they give a little insight, warm your heart, if they lighten your burdens even just for a day, then I have "made some difference," I have "mattered."

Life is Not a Destination

Acknowledgements

This page is to acknowledge the help received from others. It's in recognition of those I couldn't have done without - and a plea for forgiveness to those I have disappointed. I don't guess it interests you who read the book but it fulfills an obligation and confesses personal shortcomings.

In appreciation I should include all those who taught me about life and living, the standards and ethics by which I believe a "good" person should abide. A fella's mother and father immediately come to mind - and the memory of a Grandfather who coughed his life away after working for years in the copper mines. Then too there were a couple of wars along the way. There's nothing like the impersonal terror of war-up-close to tear the tinsel from the fundamentals of life.

For the immediate task I must thank my wife, Dorothy, for her never failing encouragement, Ms. Stacey Willey who never hesitated to tell me if I was about to screw something up and those kind folks who read and commented on my work in the past – Thank You. Responsibility for mistakes of course is mine.

Last but not least I wish to thank you folks who choose to read these pages. Without you there would be no need for any of it.

Enjoy! I hope I don't disappoint you.

Ω

Life is Not a Destination

TABLE OF CONTENTS

Life is Not a Destination

FORWARD

Life is not a destination. Life is what you do along the way. Whether you joyfully embrace or cynically reject each day, week, year as you live it, the choice is yours and yours alone.

We are born not by choice but by chance. We live our lives not by chance but by choice. And the only certainty is that we will die. That in between time is up to you. This book you're holding emphasizes and embraces the "enjoy" in between.

The book came about through the many kind comments of you folks who read my newspaper articles, magazine articles and the other books I have written. You've asked if there was a book containing some of those articles.

Many of you related memories generated by my writing. You mentioned similar situations in your own lives. You said so many nice things you "turned my head."

To those of you who were so kind, here is the book you requested. To those of you who aren't familiar with my writing I can only say it seems to come well recommended. You hold the product in your hands. Look it over. See what you think.

There are no tears here. I try to promote positive attitudes, smiles and maybe a tug or two at your heartstrings.

I hope you will enjoy.

Ω

"The game of life is not so much in holding a good hand as playing a poor hand well."

H. T. Leslie

General Stories

ALONE ON A WIDE WIDE SEA

Dorothy and I had sailed a little 21 foot MacGregor sloop, the "LeAnn," from Marquette on Lake Superior through the lakes to Chicago, down the river system past St. Louis to New Orleans and out across Lake Pontchatrain into the Gulf of Mexico. We lived on the offshore islands of the Gulf Coast – in the boat – for several weeks. We enjoyed the trip, had a lot of fun, and learned a lot about life aboard a sailboat – and about life in general.

We finally sold the "LeAnn" (She had been named after my youngest daughter) to a young couple at Fort Walton Beach, Florida.

With what we'd learned on that three-month trip, we overlaid our requirements against the balance in our bankbook and settled on a Bayfield 25 as "LeAnn's" replacement. After a bit of searching I found what we wanted in a yacht yard at Tarpon Springs, Florida.

She was a beautiful thing. She'd been sitting in dry dock, propped up on a crib, for the past two years just waiting for us. And we had been looking that long.

The owners, a nice older couple that had moved further inland, were eager to sell. An offer was made. A counter offer returned. I kept remembering things I should have checked after the time to check them had passed. She looked good, though, sitting proudly and patiently, waiting for her turn to once more grasp the wind and surge forward through the eternal sea. Patience, darlin'. It won't be long now. Finally the deal is done!

The prior owners, man and wife, courteously briefed me on quirks and techniques they had developed and modifications they had made. They then wished me fair sailing, and went their way.

Dorothy and I found a financial institution willing to gamble on our prospects and we now owned another sailboat. She was ours - Dorothy's and mine! Well, Dorothy's and mine and the bank's if you want to get technical.

The little boat had been long out of the water and was going to need a little work. "Needs a little work." All you boat owners, men and women, out there know what that expression, voiced by an eager new owner, can entail. It was going to be three weeks before "Seaclusion" (that's what we named her) would see the sea.

A couple weeks are spent refinishing the bottom, polishing the topside, patching the fuel tank, fitting an auto-pilot, and the multitude of tasks required to get provisioned and ready to "cast off" for a port in Texas.

Advice, help, and encouragement were abundant on all sides and I am grateful to the friendly folks at Flaherty's Marine; owner, employees, and fellow tenants. We were a community unto ourselves. The rest of the world should get along that well.

One day the yard lift gently carried "Seaclusion" from her cradle to the water. A short shakedown run, a few minor corrections and adjustments, and "Seaclusion" and I are ready for sea.

Dorothy is stuck in Lansing, Michigan, nose to her computer, earning money while her loving husband is away playing "Treasure Island."

The first leg of the trip was planned to go as far as Cedar Key on Florida's west coast. This was to be another "shakedown cruise" actually. I wanted to arrive at Cedar Key with plenty of daylight to "feel" my way into port. That read out to a 3:00 AM departure. Dark! Oh, well, I already knew my way out of Tarpon Springs. I can make that in the dark.

The last night ashore I had dinner with Maddy Anderson, a good and helpful friend from way back. Shelley and Roy Powell, a couple more good people, helped with transportation and storage problems. I bunk down in the focs'l 'til time to cast off.

My day started with the clattering of my old time alarm clock about 2:30 AM. The new day continued as I got lines in, tripped over things and had a heck of a time getting the boat away. The incoming tide held her broadside and fast against the pier.

If I woke anyone else, and I surely must have, they were very gracious and did not come topside and laugh at me. Neither did they see the proximity to a repeat of the Andrea Dorea disaster as I unceremoniously clawed and struggled away from the berth.

"It's O.K. Sweetheart," I patted Seaclusion's cabin top, "I'll make it up to you later."

The channel was well marked and the departure was uneventful after my harrowing "cast off" adventure. If there were any other "events" along the way it was too dark for me to see them. We rounded the final channel marker and steadied on the course of the first leg of the trip. Everything is working fine. All running lights are burning brightly. The soft binnacle light shows the compass steady on course. The friendly lights of shore are winking unconcernedly while my little single cylinder diesel inboard engine sang happily in the hold.

It's a little cool, but it's still March. Summer isn't here yet. It'll warm up when the sun comes up. Things just couldn't be going any better.

Passing a marker buoy at the end of the first leg, on course and very close to on time, I find that I'm making between four and one half and five knots. The sun is making its presence known on the eastern horizon and a gentle breeze from the south-southwest has sprung up. As soon as it's light I'll raise the sail.

It's a beautiful sunrise. How could it be otherwise? As the darkness burned away like a fog it revealed a busy ocean surface hurrying toward the northeast. A couple of seagulls passed, purposefully stroking their way to somewhere. Porpoise came by to "check me out" and continued on their rollicking way.

Up with the sails!

The autopilot holds the course well. I celebrate my achievement with a hot cup of coffee. The alcohol stove takes a little longer than the electric pot at home. So what? I'm not in a hurry.

With the sails up and drawing well I shut the engine down.

Lord, it's quiet. The occasional slap of a wave against the hull; otherwise there's only the easy motion of the boat with a gentle quartering sea and a fair wind hurrying her along.

Alone, alone, all all alone with the lonely sky and the sea. I shoulda been a poet.

I wonder how long I could stay out here? Dorothy, where are you right now? I know where you ought to be - right here with me.

A big sigh. Aaaah! It's too nice a day and place and "Seaclusion" seems too happy to be back in her own environment to feel anything but great. I wonder if I couldn't just stay out here? The heck with stopping at Cedar Key. Get out the chart. Spread it out on the galley table. Try to fit a couple charts together, match latitude and longitude, quite a juggling match. Yes! Yes, by golly! I calculate distances, courses, guess in a wind drift factor, ignore any current in this corner of the Gulf and figure fuel consumption with all intent to maximize sailing time. We will strike out for Apalachicola. Florida shoreline gradually slips below the horizon and disappears as "Seaclusion" gently lopes along, chortling through the occasional wave. I relax, read a book, or look out across the eternal sea.

It must have looked exactly like this 'way back at the dawn of time.' Sailors would venture out a little farther, and a little farther, deciding to press a bit more -just like me. Some of them thought they might fall off the edge of the world. Not like me. If I fall out of the boat out here, though, what's the difference? I prefer to think, "Just like me."

I do get up and trail about a hundred feet of propolyn line astern. Just in case. Without a safety harness to strap on it's better than nothing.

The day passes quite pleasantly. I enjoy a little snack at appropriate times thanks to the Earl of Sandwich and the inventor of peanut butter.

Porpoise never seem to tire of coming and going.

We are all having a very laid-back, slow moving and pleasant afternoon. No other boats or land in sight. Not a worry in the world.

Worry? Let's check things out. The sun is slipping toward the sea on the western horizon. A dirty gray line of clouds ahead is running from northeast to southwest. I'm not sure what the "salty" thing to call those clouds is but, in the flying business, we would call something like that a "roll cloud," preceding thunderstorms - high winds - turbulence.

There's a bit more of a sea running now, from the southwest. Six or eight foot waves, I would guess. There are two smaller wave patterns crossing at an angle to each other. All in all, "Seaclusion" is picking her way through these troubled waters a little nervously dodging this way and that. I had better prepare for the night. Those clouds don't look friendly. Better take in the sail.

The porpoise seem to have knocked off for the day too. There's just me.

The engine starts readily and the faithful auto pilot holds the course steady.

As I go forward the light is fading. Darkness comes on rapidly in the southern latitudes. We aren't really that far south, but the clouds ahead seem to have had something to do with the sudden dimming of the light.

The bow is riding up and down ten or twelve (?) feet as each sea passes, diving to port or starboard in an absolutely unpredictable manner.

I free the jib halyard at the base of the mast and move

across the foredeck to gather in the jib.

One hand for the boat, one hand for me – that's a "rule of the sea." If it isn't, it ought to be. Sometimes it's two hands for me.

It's dark now. The bow pulpit is surging around like a thing possessed. What in blazes am I doing out here - alone - in the dark - on this bucking bit of fiberglass? I think of the trailing length of line astern.

There are stars astern too. They stare down in a disinterested manner, watching this creature hanging onto sailcloth and lifelines while the sea conspires to devour him.

The last bit of sail is secured into the sail bag, the neck pulled tight and made fast to the pulpit. I do remember to secure the end of the halyard as I pass the mast on the way to the cockpit.

Clambering down into the cockpit, I sit with my back against the cabin bulkhead, braced against the pitching of the boat. Thank you, Lord.

The engine confidently growls its song while the propeller chews its way through the sea. The auto pilot drives incessantly back and forth as it is wont to do, maintaining a general direction. Everything is secure! My heart slows down. Breathing returns to normal. The steady vibration of the engine is reassuring as it drives us resolutely forward through the waves and spray.

The stars continue to watch silently from remote space. There's a feeling that I have not experienced at any other time or place in my life. There's just the stars and the sea and God and me. Thoughts of interests ashore, of day-to-day problems fade to insignificance.

Night passes slowly and uncomfortably - but not as uncomfortable as those minutes I spent hanging from the bow pulpit.

The clouds have taken away the stars. A cold rain blows horizontally through the cockpit. Have you ever noticed that, when you're in the rain, there's always that trickle of cold water that finds its way through your rain gear to your bare skin?

Dawn was a long time coming. I would go out into the cockpit with the cold rain – look around – check for whatever I could see topside. The engine growled on steadily, never missing a beat. The cross-seas kept the boat moving nervously in an unpredictable manner. The autopilot continued to cycle back and forth correcting for the seas while the boat and I moved steadily to the northwest.

On one trip topside I sighted the stern light of another boat proceeding southeast. Well, at least we didn't collide.

Between lookout trips I tried to get a little rest. I sat in the galley jammed between the hull and a bulkhead to keep the uncertain roll of the boat from dumping me on the deck. It was a long night.

As the east lightened my topside checks revealed that, through luck or good planning, all remained secure even though the weather hadn't eased at all. It was too rough to prepare the ham and eggs breakfast I had planned. It was peanut butter sandwiches and water.

About noon we passed several shrimp boats, anchored, riding out the weather or waiting for whatever shrimp boats wait for.

By four that afternoon we sighted land. My course had been set to reach the "government cut" through the offshore islands into Apalachicola Bay. I was only off by about a half mile. Christopher Columbus didn't hit it any closer than that.

Fuel was down to next to nothing minus and less than that. Just through the cut the little diesel hacked and coughed and quit. I scrambled forward again and got the anchor out. I was able to raise the marina at Apalachicola who agreed to send out five gallons of diesel fuel. I did have to wait – they were still a few miles away – but I caught a nap and don't even remember how long it took. The guy pulled alongside and passed me the can of fuel. "Pay us when you get in," he shouted and was gone.

There was a little twisting and standing on my head and such to prime the engine but we got 'er done.

We – when I say "we," I mean "Seaclusion" and I - made it to the mooring at Apalachicola and, tied up. I stumbled ashore to a shower – that had no hot water - and fell into my bunk back aboard. "Seaclusion" lay peacefully, no longer pitching about like a thing possessed.

About ten hours of sleep and a hot "store bought" breakfast put a brighter hue on life in general. I settled my bill and set out to motor along the protected intercoastal waterway. Just keep out of the way of the tugboats and their barges and it was most pleasant, leisurely and relaxed cruise. All was well.

When I reached Pirate's Cove on the Alabama – Florida line I arranged a berth for the boat and tied 'er up. Dorothy, I'm coming home!

There is, however, a new inscription lettered on Seaclusion's Companionway hatch:

"Thy Sea is so Great, my Boat is so Small"

♎

Life is Not a Destination

STAY WITH THE HAPPY PEOPLE

Here's a situation I got involved in. I'm sure many of you have similar experiences. I'd been dealing with a fella who started "toe-dancing" around an agreement we had. Not wanting to abandon the relationship I bent and twisted and turned in an attempt to salvage the arrangement. Several months passed and it didn't resolve itself. The other guy undoubtedly has his side of this disagreement so we won't pursue it further.

An analysis of the situation would reveal that I entered too eagerly into a relationship I hadn't fully analyzed. There's a few dollars involved but I have to realize they're gone. Accepting that, is it worth the recrimination, the anger, the trouble? Experience is a hard teacher. First it gives the test – then it teaches the lesson. My judgment was bad and it cost me.

How long do I make myself pay? And it is I who is now making me pay. A few lines from a Robert Service poem come to mind: "The thought comes back of an ancient wrong and it stings like a frozen lash. The urge arose, to kill! to kill! . . ." The money is gone. Accept that. There's nothing more that can be done. A person has to put it behind them. But every time it comes to mind "it stings like a frozen lash."

I'm doing that to myself, aren't I? If you think about

it, they call psychiatrists for people who continue to intentionally injure themselves. I believe the human body automatically generates chemicals called "peptides" or "neurotoxins" or "adrenalin" or whatever the term is. Your whole system automatically reacts to your mental state. That's why high-pressure executives – and some of the rest of us too – get "up-tight," generate excess stomach acid and give ourselves ulcers. It's not an easy thing to do – revenge would seem sweet – but the price you make yourself pay is too high. Turn to the happy people. Concentrate on the happy people. There are a lot of happy people out there.

When things are going along as we feel they should we remain pretty much unaware of the details. It's when something goes wrong, a car cuts you off at an intersection, someone steps ahead of you in line, the guy (or girl) at the next table is loud and using profanity, these draw your attention. The folks who hold open a door for you, who say "please" and "thank you," who go through life obeying the rules, that's the way it's supposed to be. These "happy people" are not as apparent as the others. Turn away from the bums. Go with the happy people.

Here's another scenario that has played out in my travels down life's road. I've written a couple books and I peddle them wherever I can. I go to festivals and art shows and street fairs. I set up my little stand and enjoy meeting and greeting and talking to folks, grown ups and children, all having a good time.

I'm sometimes asked to speak to school kids. At one class, I had read a story from one of my books. The class and I seemed to be getting along very well. A youngster came up and wanted to buy one of my books. "For my daddy," the student said. The child dug deep into a pocket and brought out a handful of coins. I watched as the coins were fingered and sorted and counted. And what do you know! There was just enough to buy that book. I autographed the book "To (daddy)." I hope "daddy" enjoys my book half as much as I did doing business with his child.

An old necktie was on my mind as I transacted that book sale. I've never worn that necktie. I had it cleaned and pressed and encased in protective cellophane. It probably cost more to clean and press that necktie than it cost new. You see it was my three-year-old daughter, living with her momma down in Texas, who bought me that necktie. She was at a rummage sale with her momma. She picked out the necktie and got her momma to buy it - "for daddy."

That daughter has children of her own now but I still have that necktie. It hangs on my office wall. I look at it whenever the world appears a little dark. I couldn't help but remember that necktie as that child was counting the change. He had "just enough" to buy the book.

Yes, you cynics out there, I did have an ulterior motive. I kind of believe that somewhere records are being kept on each of us. One day we're going to have to answer for what we've done along life's path. When that time comes and an old heathen like me digs down deep in his pocket, I hope I can come up with "just enough."

Another of life's sunnier incidents and I'll let you go. At a book sale at an art fair one day a woman stopped by the booth. She spent some time looking at one of my books. She confessed that she wanted to buy the book but she didn't have any money – at least not with her. I gave her the book and said, "mail me a check."

Have I gotten short changed in any of these dealings? It depends on what you mean by "short changed." The secret of staying happy is to think of that grade school child who wanted a book "for daddy." Remember the woman who wanted a book but didn't have enough money with her. The contrast is – what? Oh! I guess I forgot to tell you about that woman. Two days after that book fair I got a check in the mail along with a beautiful "thank you" note. The thank you note was worth more to me than the check. It's a human failing that we're more inclined to cling fast to wrongs that have been done us than we are to remember the "please" and "thank you" and the person who held the door. There's not a pill you can take or some social condition on which you can blame things. You have to take the responsibility for your own life. Nobody can do it for you. It's something you have to learn to control yourself.

Keep a happy thought. Don't let the stomach acid get you.

♎

CIVILIAN CONSERVATION CORPS

(l-r) A.J. "Swede" Anderson, Gerry McGlue, Arne Nyman, Romeo Carafelly, Albin Zigila

They had gathered to erect a memorial to "the old days." Memories hearkened back to 1933, back to the hard times of the great depression. There was very little work. Unemployment was widespread. There wasn't a job to be had for love nor money. Soup kitchens were a fact of life. Families were going hungry. The number one song on the hit parade was: "Brother, Can You Spare a Dime." Here are a few words from the chorus:

> "Once I built a railroad, I made it run,
> Made it race against time.
> Once I built a railroad, now it's done —
> Brother, can you spare a dime?"

Franklin Delano Roosevelt had been elected President of these United States and began initiating programs to try to alleviate this condition. Among these many government employment schemes was one called the Civilian Conservation Corps, the CCC. The thrust of this program, in addition to putting young men to work, was to restore and preserve our nation's natural resources, and - coincidentally – to restore pride in those young men. They would be able to work, earn a little money.

To be eligible for the CCC program a man had to be in good health, between the ages of 18 and 25, have little or no income and a family on welfare. That's what they used to call it back then; welfare.

Additionally, if a family was on welfare and had a healthy male between the ages of 18 and 25, he went to work in the CCC or the family lost its welfare check. Period. There was no appeal. If someone in that age group and situation got into trouble with the police they were given a choice: to the CCC - or to jail. The CCC job paid $30 a month. The guy only got five dollars of that for himself. The rest was sent to his family. One of the CCC camps, camp # 690, was built near Alder Creek in Big Bay in Upper Michigan. The camp number was later changed to 3627 for whatever reasons.

Gerry McGlue of L'Anse joined. A train took him to Marquette. He was familiar with Marquette as he had spent four years in an orphanage there. In spite of his familiarity with Marquette – or maybe because of it - he missed the train that was to take him to the CCC camp at Big Bay. He wanted that job. He knew his family needed the income. Gerry headed down the tracks and walked the 25 miles to Big Bay.

A.J. "Swede" Anderson from Skanee joined up in Ironwood. He came by train all the way, "The DSS&A (Duluth, South Shore and Atlantic) from Ironwood," he says – "and the LS&I (Lake Superior and Ishpeming) to Big Bay."

Romeo Carafelly was a kid wandering the streets down in Detroit. He heard that the CCC fed three meals a day. He was barely getting two – if he was lucky. The train took him to Chicago, another carried him on to Marquette – and the LS&I to Big Bay.

Arne Nyman was an Ishpeming teenager. The family was on welfare. The man said, "Get your gear, son, you're going." He ran home. No one was there. He stuffed his toothbrush, some baking powder and twenty cents into his pocket. He left a note: "Gone to the CCC" – and headed for Big Bay.

Albin Zigila was another kid walking the streets of Detroit and in as bad shape as all the rest. He decided he would join the CCC. He was 16 years old. The guy

who signed him up said he had to be 18. He said he was
18. He was sent to Big Bay.

At the CCC camp the day started at 6:00 AM.
Breakfast was at 7:00. By 8:00 they were in the trucks
and on their way into the woods. Among other tasks
they brushed out the gooseberry bushes. Gooseberries
were a host for the bugs that give white pine blister rust.
They built a road, today called the "Triple A," across the
Yellow Dog plains to a place called Anderson's corner,
a sort of wood cutting farm family site, and beyond.
They then built the Panorama Fire Tower and erected a
20 mile phone line.

Another task was to rebuild "Cement Gust"
Anderson's dam on the outlet of Lake Independence
- and add a fish ladder. They mapped the bottoms of
Lake Independence and Saux Head Lake about ten miles
south. They also fought forest fires, built more roads,
cleaned roadways, did whatever they were told. The
United States Army supervised the CCC camps so these
young men also learned discipline! They weren't there
to picnic; they were there to work!

For light at night they had kerosene lamps. Their
recreation was a room with a pool table. There was no
electricity, no radio and no work on Sunday. Al and Jerry
and Swede and the rest - there were a couple hundred
of them – earned their $30 a month. The other $25 was
sent to their families.

I asked Swede what he thought of his time in the
CCC. "It was 19 fun months. That started my career

in the woods. I'm retired now from the 'American Corporation.' I was their Woodlands Superintendent."

Gerry's answer, "I think it was the cat's meow!"

Arne shrugged and answered, ". . . was proud to be helping my family. . . was a good start for my young life."

Romeo said he was getting three square meals a day and grinned. "Everything was beautiful."

"I could have been in jail." Al shook his head, "We learned the work ethic."

The CCC certainly set these four guys on the right path. Sitting with these "old soldiers" from that war on poverty I thought how much we owe to them too. Loggers are cutting the second or third growth of the trees the CCC planted some seventy years ago. We're traveling today on their woods roads; crossing the bridges they built and enjoying the park they established at Isle Royale. The forest fires, the blister rust, what else? There were nearly three million of those young recruits nationwide.

Their conversations as they reminisced were illuminating: "You know that guy, the boxer." "Yeah! Always fooling with his hair." A shake of the head, "His elevator didn't go quite to the top." "What was the name of that bar? The one in hungry hollow?" "Remember the songs?" "No, no, don't sing 'em here. There are ladies."

And there were ladies at the dedication.. Ms. Vernice Temple of Big Bay who actively assisted Albin Zigila, a promoting member of the Michigan Chapter of the National Association of Civilian Conservation Corps Alumni. They were going to erect a small wooden sign, a memento on the site of the old CCC camp. Ms. Pat Gruber, Manager of the Longyear Realty Land Operations that now owned the property gave permission to erect the sign on Longyear land. Officer Dennis Nezich of the Michigan Department of Natural Resources helped. He dug the holes for the posts. Harry Bourgeois from Big Bay was there too. Harry was a CCC alumnus from a camp over at Watersmeet in western Upper Michigan. There were wives too and friends made along the way all seated with and among them. They were all survivors, veterans of the hard times who had earned their right to participate in the ceremony. They put up a modest marker, a wooden sign beside the road: It's still there. There may be brush around it, somebody's car parked in front of it, but if you look, it's still there: "CCC Camp Big Bay."

♎

*"Do what you can,
with what you have,
where you are."*

Theodore Roosevelt

AURORA, THE GODDESS OF DAWN

It was 1:00 o'clock - in the morning. I'd been puttsing around in my little office, peering at the computer screen, pressing various buttons, and wondering why the cotton pickin' thing wouldn't do what I wanted it to do.

By the way, those of you who fool with computers, isn't it strange that the best way to "fix" the thing - is to shut it down - turn it off - and start it up again? Whoop-dee-doo! It works well! There are times when I wish I could do that with myself. There's gotta be some philosophy in there somewhere.

Back to 1:00 o'clock in the morning: I had brushed my teeth and was stumbling bleary eyed toward bed. I noticed it was unusually light outside. The light seemed to be coming from the northern horizon. I thought it might be city lights reflecting on clouds, you know how they do. But the light was from out over Lake Superior. There aren't any cities - or lights - out there. There were no clouds that night either. I went to the window to investigate this strange phenomenon. There were the lights! They moved. They swayed back and forth. While I watched a shaft of light leapt straight up into the night sky - and stood there - a "pillar of light." The best I could tell Moses wasn't around anywhere nor were there any voices speaking to me. The base of that curtain of light wavered like a snake, turning from pale green to gold to bright orange. It twisted and turned and folded back upon itself, following no particular pattern. Lord, it was beautiful!

I grabbed the telephone and called my sister who lived next door. My brother-in-law, Don Salo, answered with a concerned sounding "Hello?" Phone calls in the middle of the night do not normally announce that you have just won the Publisher's Clearinghouse Sweepstakes. Late night calls do not usually bear good news.

"Get up! Go out and look at the Northern Lights," I blurted.

"Huh? Wha? Well – yeah - OK."

I hung up. Maybe he won't know who it was. (Fat chance!)

When I got back to the window, the reds and

golds had faded. That great vertical shaft of light had dimmed some too but was still there. Then the aurora brightened again, glowed for a little bit, twisted feebly, and faded.

I haven't seen Don since that call. I don't know if we're still speaking to one another or not.

That aurora - or Northern Lights - is one of the wonders of the far north (and south) country and sometimes reaches our Upper Peninsula. It comes in the dark, in the stillness of the night. There's no noise, no announcement of its coming. It may glow just a little. If you're not in a dark area, somewhere isolated from the lights of town, you may not even see it. Then again it may fill the whole sky with a spectacular display of shimmering, changing, rippling light. The spectacle was named "Aurora" after the Greek goddess of the dawn. Aurora, it was said, would drive her steeds bearing her glowing solar chariot over the horizon, scattering the tender, rose colored rays of the approaching day before her. She is the mother of the winds, of the soft breeze and of the raging storm. She is a thing of awe and beauty.

Scientists have analyzed, gathered data, and formulated explanations of these lights in the polar skies, this "Aurora Borealis." There's one down south too - called the "Aurora Australis." They say the light in the sky is caused by sunspot activity. Sun spots are huge hydrogen explosions on the surface of the sun that generate electromagnetic particles that then travel through space on a solar wind. Those particles passing near earth are captured by the earth's magnetic field that surrounds us. The particles are concentrated, gathered in the area nearest to the earth's magnetic poles and are often seen southward down to 20 or 25 degrees of latitude. Leave it to scientists to take the romance and mystery out of things.

Statistics on the aurora would indicate there's an 11-year cycle of maximum activity. The aurora, they say, will most often occur around the time of the equinox. The equinox is when the sub-point, the point on the earth directly below the sun is crossing the earth's equator. That would put aurora activity most active in March through April and September through October. The colors of the light are affected by the magnetic particle reaction with atomic oxygen (whatever that is) that causes a green glow. Molecular nitrogen, which is also contained in the atmosphere, glows red. And then the scientists get involved in discussing altitudes and particle dispersion and the effect it has on radio communication.

There was a widespread power failure not too long ago in southeast Canada and the northeast United States. When they got things working again the power failure was attributed to a particularly large surge of magnetic particles in those solar winds. The magnetic fields they created were strong enough to affect the power in the electric transmission lines blowing out transformers and other critical components. That sort of thing takes the romance out of it.

I remember back when it was thought that the northern lights were caused by the reflection of the sun on polar glaciers and icebergs. They were beams of light created by Aurora driving her solar chariot over the horizon. The scattered rosy-hued rays she scattered before her were refracted, bent by the polar ice formations to arc high into the sky. That explanation may not have been "scientific," but it was a lot more soul satisfying.

Can't you just visualize four prancing white chargers abreast with a beautiful golden haired Aurora in a flowing white toga driving them forward? Then the scientific minded analysts place this beautiful phenomenon on an impersonal dissecting table where it's seen as nothing more than a cold and lifeless cadaver. When I see a beautiful sunrise or watch the northern lights dance in the midnight sky I don't think solar particles. I think, "Aurora!"

Now, if I can just figure some way to get back in the good graces of my brother-in-law . . .

Life is Not a Destination

PLEASE? - THANK YOU

The patient made himself comfortable. The psychiatrist asked, "What seems to be the problem?"

"I don't know. I seem to make people angry - fathead!"

That's a joke. At least, it's supposed to be. There are few people, other than Dirty Harry, the tough movie cop character, who would intentionally do that. "Dirty Harry" was a popular movie. Why? I suspect there are a lot of us who secretly would like to hide our real selves in a character like that - with a big (figuratively speaking) "gun" to blow all our troubles away. "Go ahead! Make my day!" But that's make-believe. That fantasy is the reason we go to movies. Life - real life - is a mirror. It reflects what you show it.

You're driving down the street. Someone suddenly pulls in front of you. It upsets you and you blow your horn. The other driver points at you (with other than his index finger). You both drive off. Your guts churn for a bit. That's usually as far as it goes. There have been cases where one of the guys in a traffic situation pulled out a pistol and shot the other fella'.

Suppose you're hurrying down the aisle in a department store. Someone, their attention elsewhere, looking at merchandise or whatever, suddenly steps in front of you. Maybe you bump into one another. "Sorry, I didn't see you." "My fault. I wasn't looking." No harm done. There's a smile on both sides. "Have a good day." "You too." You each go your own way. Or maybe you ignore each other. Maybe one of you mumbles something under their breath. Bad feelings. There's no "happy ending." It only takes a few seconds and a little consideration to be polite. It doesn't cost a thing. It's a win win situation.

There's a price to pay in the wear and tear irritation creates in your body. The chemicals that automatically flush into your blood stream in response to your mental attitude strain the organs of your body. That's what tension, a hostile mental attitude, even momentary anger generates. "I'm sorry" or "Excuse me" is the way to go even when you feel it was the other person's fault. The car incident and the people situation are the same. In the car what's a visual sign for "Oops! Sorry, I didn't see you," or "My fault. I wasn't looking"? Wouldn't it be great if there were one?

However you might look at it, don't take these trivial things personally. That guy (or girl) in the other car didn't plan it. They didn't lay in wait, chuckling, gloating in anticipation over pulling out in front of you. Maybe it was a stupid move. Did your calling attention to it by blowing the horn help? No! It embarrassed them especially if they, too, recognize it as a stupid thing to do. They feel they must defend themselves. They feel they must retaliate. They were wrong - then you were wrong. It's a no-win situation. It was (enter your own description) in which no one was injured – unless you allow it to upset you. Forget it! Apply that same approach, that same philosophy to so many of the otherwise upsetting situations every day.

Some of you may know this - or not. Animals in the woods are a whole lot smarter in their relationships than we are. They eat. They sleep. They get amorous in season. Their egos don't suffer injury. They know themselves! Maybe they just know instinctively but they know. You won't see an animal "taking revenge," except in the movies and we all know those are make-believe. A bear walking through the woods doesn't say, "Did you see that @$% chipmunk cut right out in front of me? I won't let him get away with that. I'll . . ." That sort of response is nonproductive and the bear instinctively knows that. The bear won't waste the time or the effort.

I read somewhere that the things we're most afraid of are the things we don't understand. I think "ourselves" is something we don't understand. Each of us, deep down inside where nobody sees is fragile. We're afraid of being exposed for what we, deep down inside, know about ourselves. We try to hide it by covering it with a hard shell - as when you "point" with the wrong finger.

We all want to be loved or admired or respected or understood - all of the above. It'll never really happen until we have a glimmer of understanding of ourselves.

Cruelty, in remarks as well as actions, is the "hiding" tool of the weak, the ignorant. Expect consideration, caring, tenderness only from a person with strong character. Children are often more transparent but the logic is the same. When you see an adult do something, and wonder why, ask yourself why a child would have done it. You'll probably have the answer.

John Wayne, in one of his movies said, "Never apologize. It's a sign of weakness." Forgive me, Duke, but you were <u>wrong</u>. It's a sign of strength. "Please." "Thank You." "Pardon Me." These expressions are the oil, the lubricant that promotes, accelerates, and smooths the bumpy ride of human relations. Throw in "I'm Sorry" and "You're Welcome" now and then too.

All this won't set you up for "high tea" with the Queen of England, but it'll make your day go more smoothly - guaranteed. So remember: "Please," "Thank you," "Pardon me" fathead.

Good ole Boys

"ME 'N CARL"

Carl was my uncle and I loved him. The first job I ever had was working for Carl back in the 1940s when I was maybe 14 years old. He ran a gasoline station on the south side of town. That experience must have had something to do with making me the person I am. I guess all our experiences have something to do with shaping us. Either way working with and for Carl has left me with some of the fondest memories I've gathered along life's road.

I probably ought to tell you a little about Carl. He became my uncle when he married my mother's sister, Jean. Jean was a good lookin' woman but – well – I guess the gentlest way to say it is that she had an agenda of her own. Lord help you if you crossed her. We'll get more into that later in the story.

Carl's daddy – his name was Carl also - had been in several businesses along the way. While Carl was still an impressionable teenager, his dad was involved in bootlegging whiskey. From about 1919 'til it was repealed in 1933 the Volstead act was the law of the land. During that time the sale or consumption of alcoholic beverages was banned. That was the law – and that was that – well, that was supposed to be that.

There were people who didn't go along with that law. Booze, like so many things that are "forbidden," only seemed to make it more attractive. Those folks whose philosophy differed were willing to pay a premium price to continue to imbibe – "on the sly." Isn't this the very heart of the capitalistic system at work? There was a demand. There was no supply. The demand side was very, well, demanding. That meant there was premium buck to be made. Satisfying that nationwide thirst came to be called "bootlegging," "moonshining" and even led to the making of "bathtub gin."

The term bootlegging, I am told, came from away back in colonial times. The fellas who would make and deliver liquor weren't always too eager to pay the government levied tax. To smuggle this non-tax-paid booze they had to hide it. Riding on a horse, as they did in those days, didn't provide many hiding places. Horsemen wore tall boots back then and these "bootleggers" would slip a flat pint or so size bottle or two – or three - down inside their boot, hence, "Bootlegger."

"Moonshine" was a naturally adapted expression

from the fact that the illegal liquor was made in hidden places many times by the light of the moon. "Bathtub Gin," so named because – well it's obvious isn't it? By whatever name it was illegal booze smuggled to folks who still wanted a drink.

Carl was a good-looking young fellow with a ready smile and a winning personality – "charisma" they call it. When I worked with him he was still a good ole' boy and hadn't lost the charm. Back in the "dry" days another of his endearing qualities was his ability to readily produce a drink - at dances, social functions, lodge hall meetings or casually on the street corner. He was a ready source and could deliver almost immediately.

His "social importance" probably had something to do with the attraction he held for my aunt. I'm sure she enjoyed her share of attention in his popularity while Carl, on the other hand, was just a regular good ole' boy. He was an outdoorsman, adventurous and attracted to deeds of daring do – motorcycles, speedboats, (the illegal booze of course) and all that sort of thing.

I probably should also mention here that, in these later years Carl retained a taste for booze. I would politely say he drank a little more than he should have but aah, shucks, I gotta be honest with you: Carl drank a whole lot more than he should have. I don't know if he'd qualify as an alcoholic in those days but he was sure in the runnin'.

Carl, being what he was, attracted a bunch of other good ole' boys. Fellas who like to tip a jug seem to be like members of a fraternity. They just naturally seem to be attracted to one another. I don't know what in their lives or natures inclined them that way. Another of my uncles, Joe DeCook (husband of another of my mother's sisters) had a theory of his own. He once said that he, Joe, would take a drink because he liked the taste of the drink while Carl would have a drink because he craved its after effect. I had my own idea about Carl's addiction. I often thought that if I was married to Jean I just might - well, enough about that. My theory almost seems to dovetail into Uncle Joe's theory, doesn't it?

Anyway, those good ole' boys who became regulars would often spend hours sitting on oil cases or a board we had laid on top of the steam radiator or just lounging on the bale of waste rags in the corner. And they knew that buried deep in those rags would usually be a pint bottle of whiskey. It wouldn't be expensive aged-in-the-wood booze. Carl's favorite brand was called "PM," inexpensive – cheap, know what I mean? "Polish Moonlight" the regulars called it for reasons I could only imagine. There were many a good yarn spun by those good ole' boys and an impressionable young fella like me eagerly soaked them up.

But let's jump back to the prohibition days for a minute. This story is typical of the tales the good ole' boys would relate over dinner pail lunch or sitting around waiting for business.

Carl's dad used to get the illegal booze wherever he could. The stories never got into that too much. Young

Carl was one of his most productive outlets. Carl's personality made him popular in any group and the booze just added to it. At local dances people would sidle up to Carl. There'd be a brief conversation in low tones, a couple dollars would change hands and Carl would disappear – but not for long. In the corner a brown paper bag would emerge from under his shirt, surreptitiously change hands and the deed was done.

The police may – or may not – have been actively pursuing these goings on. Whatever the case you have to remember it was Carl and his cronies who were telling the stories. Carl said he had been stopped by suspicious police officers on several occasions but they never found any evidence. Here's what Carl claimed his secret was. The automobiles back in those days had those skinny balloon tires with inner tubes. Carl and his dad would let the air out of the tire, fill the inner tube half way or so with the booze, then they'd pump air back into the tire 'til it was hard as a rock – way over normal tire pressure. When Carl arrived at the dance or wherever the folks were gathered, he'd park off in the shadows somewhere. He'd always make sure to have at least one tire with the air valve on the bottom. When someone had a request Carl would slip out to where he'd parked the car checking carefully to see that he hadn't been followed or wasn't being watched. Then he'd crouch down and hold the open bottle or jar or whatever container up to that air valve. By tripping the valve the air pressure would force the booze out and fill the container.

The point of the story seemed to be that he was outsmarting the police – and maybe he was. The thing I always wondered – but never asked - was what did that stuff taste like. I'm sure that after being sloshed around in that automobile tire it didn't acquire the flavor of charred oak? People must have been awfully thirsty. Anyway, he was my uncle and I loved him.

We used to close the station each evening about six o'clock. Aunt Jean would come by with her car and we'd all go home. They'd drop me off on their way. By six o'clock each day Carl always had had something to drink. Some days it was more than on others. He seemed able to handle it well and, unless you knew him – or were close enough to catch his breath - the average person might not notice. But then there were other days when the whole world could tell - from clear across the street. On those days there were times when Jean would just lose it completely. On those days we'd all run for cover.

Typically Jean would come in, quickly take in the situation, and – if there were no strangers around - verbally light into Carl. She would bitterly remind him of the many evenings she had taken him home to "sleep it off." She would have to sit alone in their big beautiful home on the shore of Lake Superior. She had a valid point. Another part of their problem, I believe, was that Carl wanted children and Jean – well – that didn't seem to be a part of her plan. But that's something else again and I'd better stick to pumpin' gasoline and washing windshields.

On this particular evening Jean came by to pick us up. Carl was out of it, out there among the planets. Jean unloaded on him. In her frustration she went even further. She was well versed on where Carl stashed his jugs. She stalked over to the ragbag, rummaged around and pulled out the half empty pint bottle of PM. She marched to the rear door of the station, stepped out on the little concrete porch, removed the cap from the bottle and poured what was left out onto the ground. Carl watched with the countenance of a politician who has just lost an election. The empty bottle was ceremoniously thrown into the bushes – where it smashed against the multitude of other bottles she had thrown there in the past.

Returning, she marched across the grease room, across the wash rack, and reached behind the curved tin water tank we used to find leaks in inner tubes. When she straightened up she held another of Carl's precious stash. It followed the path of the PM. There was a bottle behind the oil drum and another behind the air compressor in the basement. Nothing escaped her.

During this "search and destroy" activity Carl looked at me with his big sad eyes and said, "Benny, if you ever get married," he slowly shook his head from side to side and added, "DON'T!" After this ceremony was completed and I had locked the door, we got in the car and went home.

The next morning Jean and Carl picked me up. No reference was made to the night before. We drove to the station; Jean dropped us off and continued on uptown to the Post Office where she worked. Carl waved goodbye as a good husband should, unlocked the door and our day had begun. In keeping with his usual procedure he headed for the ragbag and reached down for his morning picker-upper. Puzzled, he paused, dug deeper, rummaged around. Nothing! He quickly headed to the oil drum, reaching behind it. Still nothing! The air compressor, the water tank, all came up dry. The bitter truth became apparent – this was a desert! There was no drink anywhere!

We went on about opening for business, servicing the one or two early risers who needed gasoline. After a couple hours another of the "good ole' boys" stopped by, probably looking for an eye opener himself. This ole' boy was a big fella and, of course, everyone called him "Tiny." Tiny drove a gasoline delivery truck for a competing oil company but among the good ole' boys fraternity, this held no significance.

Carl was elated. He met Tiny at the door. Heads together, they conversed briefly. The conversation brought a shocked look to Tiny's face. They spoke some more in low tones. A few dollars changed hands. Tiny hurried back to his truck and drove off.

Carl and I busied ourselves with this and that. Business began to come in. Someone wanted their car greased. Someone else had a slow leak in a tire and chose to wait while we repaired it. Now and then the alarm bell would alert us that someone had driven up to the gasoline pumps requiring service. It got busy.

In the middle of all this activity Tiny returned. He parked his truck to one side and sort of slunk into the station, one hand held under his shirt. He carefully glanced around before casually sidling over to the ragbag. With no one noticing he slipped a brown paper bag down among the rags. He glanced around once more, a satisfied look on his face and walked over to the radiator to take a seat and wait.

It was turning into a good day with more and more business coming and going keeping us occupied. As usual a few people lounged around talking about the weather and this and that and passing the time of day. It was not uncommon for folks to buy a dollar's worth of gasoline (over five gallons back in those days) and stick around to discuss politics, the weather, tell a joke, and socialize.

Carl was as nervous as a long-tailed cat in a room full of rocking chairs. Tiny, still seated on the radiator, was getting a bit antsy himself. Finally Carl almost pushed the last customer out the door. Tiny was leaning forward in anticipation. As that last customer drove away Carl and Tiny lost no time getting to the ragbag.

Tiny reached down, felt around and retrieved the pint bottle. PM! What else? He held it high, grinning in anticipation. Then he handed it to Carl who, of course, had paid for it. Carl held it up to the light, peering through the amber liquid in joyful anticipation. Lowering the bottle, holding it now in both hands, he twisted the cap so as to break the seal. With the cap removed he smiled broadly and once more held the bottle up to the light. Then - there is a protocol among the good ole' boys you know - he magnanimously held the bottle out to Tiny, that he, Tiny, should have the first drink. Tiny repeated the hold-the-bottle-aloft ritual, anticipating that first drink.

In the meantime Carl discovered he had a rag tangled in the button on his shirtsleeve. He tried unsuccessfully to untangle it. In frustration he jerked at the rag. The rag and button came loose. Carl's arm flew up striking Tiny's arm. Tiny wasn't ready for that. The pint bottle of golden amber "Polish Moonlight" flew from Tiny's grasp. It arced over the accessory counter and shattered into a million pieces on the concrete floor.

Carl and Tiny stared down in shocked disbelief. Their last and best friend had just dropped dead in front of them.

I couldn't contain myself. I burst out laughing so hard I fell off the radiator. Tiny rushed toward me across the room with what I feared might be murder in his eye. I was able to slip out the door and run as fast as I could away from the station. I didn't stop 'til I was up the road a half a block or so. It was only a minute or two 'til Tiny came out, got in his truck and drove off. I kind of wandered back to the station pretending to be working at other things and sort of blended back in.

Tiny was back in short order. It had been a repeat of the earlier mission. Fortunately for Tiny and Carl, I guess, there was no one around. With a bit more care the culmination of their anticipation was achieved. Tiny even bought a coke for me. Coke sold for a nickel via a bottle dispenser in a chest type cooler. All was again well among the good ole' boys. No hard feelings. That's how things were with the good ole' boys.

Ω

"I don't like to commit myself about heaven and hell – you see I have friends in both places."

Mark Twain

Life is Not a Destination

FOGHORN IN THE NIGHT

As a kid I remember listening to Marquette's foghorn, calling out to ships unseen. The night would be dark, damp; maybe a cold drizzling rain would be falling. It was the kind of night when you felt that skullduggery could well be afoot. I'd be safe at home in a warm bed, imagination running free, listening. That low-toned "hoooonk" sounded regularly, reassuringly in the darkness.

An aid to navigation, it's called. Foghorns are used, along with lights and bells and whistles, to help those who go down to the sea in ships to find their way. I have "been there - done that," as the soda pop commercials say.

It's pretty lonely out there on a dark and foggy sea. There's no one there but you and God and the silence. Anything that reaches out to help is welcomed.

Modern ships have expensive radar and long-range navigation (Loran) and Global Positioning Satellites (GPS) to fix their location to within a few feet. But those things, as I said, cost money. There are still a lot of us "hip-pocket" sailors around that can't afford some of that equipment. We've got to rely on the same basic navigation Christopher Columbus used; "Dead Reckoning," they call it. Actually dead reckoning is the basis of all navigation - even the modern stuff. That name sure has a morbid ring to it though.

My dad owned a 28-foot cabin cruiser, a motorized lifeboat off of a World War II "Liberty" ship. He had a cabin built onto it and named it the "Sandra," after my sister. He had hired a guy part-time to take fishing parties out in it but we used it to go cruising on Lake Superior.

On this morning we left Marquette headed for Isle Royal, an island that is also a National Park, clear across Lake Superior near the Canadian shore. We were barely out of sight of land when we ran into fog. The crew was made up of Dad and I, Mike Dooley and Werner Wyland, a couple of policemen who worked with dad, and Clarence Hogan, a baker and a friend who worked at a local bakery. They were a fun crew, good fellas, every one.

To navigate we relied on the basic dead reckoning. We had a compass and a chart. That was it. Dad would set the throttle "by feel", guessing at the engine RPM (revolutions per minute). Knowing the speed at which a boat's engine turned, the number of revolutions per minute of the boat's propeller would be known also (sometimes the engine drove the propeller through a reduction gear – the propeller turned slower). With the compass he could "point" the boat at the desired course. There must be considerations at times for wind or current but the fundamentals here are sufficient to understand the principle.

So many RPM should provide so much speed. If the speed was six miles per hour and the heading was north, after an hour, you and the boat should be six miles north of where you were.

There were "crutches" we had discovered aboard the "Sandra" we used to help. The power setting, for example: We would advance the power until a steering cable running to the rudder along the boat hull would vibrate. This is called a "sympathetic vibration," in resonance with a vibration in the engine. At that particular power setting the engine and the propeller were turning at a rate to give us six miles per hour. We could also - - oh, never mind. You get enough of the drift of how things were done. It's not that important to dig deeper and we tend to wander from the story.

Dad had noted the time we passed the breakwater light northbound. We continued to run on course, keeping watch on the time, heading for Manitou Island on the tip of the Keweenaw Peninsula.

When we had run out the time we were at Manitou Island – we hoped as we couldn't see anything through the fog. We thought we were. We strained our eyes, peering into the thick fog but could see nothing! Dad shut down the engine.

Clarence came up from below where he had been making coffee – Clarence, with his baking experience, was our official cook. He'd heard the engine throttle back and came up to see why.

"Where are we," he asked?

A shrug of the shoulders. Somebody, speaking low replied for all of us: "I dunno."

Clarence eyes widened. He looked around, suddenly concerned. Dad having shut the engine down completely didn't add to Clarence's feeling of security.

It was deathly quiet. The silence boomed in our ears. Water slapped gently against the hull as the boat lost forward motion.

Worried, Clarence asked, "What did ya do . . ?"

Dad raised his hand for silence, listening. Water slurped against the hull.

"Ain't there a foghorn on Manitou?" This last from Werner.

Dad just nodded, still listening intently.

"Well I sure don't hear it."

We drifted for several minutes, straining to hear – anything, any sound at all.

Dad shook his head. "We should be there."

"Well, we ain't." No one moved. Silence!

Dad reached over to restart the engine saying, "We'll run another 15 minutes, then check again."

Clarence was developing worry wrinkles and a slight shade of green to go with them.

Fifteen minutes later we stopped the engine again; same procedure, same result.

We then elected to turn left ninety degrees from our course and run fifteen minutes more. By turning perpendicular to our course and running another fifteen minutes we were beginning a search pattern. The next turn would be another 90 degree left turn, another fifteen minutes, then another 90 degree turn, this time for 30 minutes and continuing until the pattern ran us into (that is, close enough to see) Manitou Island – or see something?

We ran 15 minutes, stopped, shut off the engine, listened. Nothing!

We turned left to run the next leg, running for another - no wait! Mike, up on the bow, waved his arms and shouted, "Stop!"

Dad quickly shifted the propeller into reverse and brought the boat to a standstill.

"Shut 'er down!" Mike called. "Listen!"

Silence! Everyone including Clarence was listening. In the silence we could all hear the distinct slapping of waves breaking on rocks. It sounded like it was just ahead, to the lef - - er - - on the port bow. (Got to stick to "salty" nautical terminology.)

We had come upon Manitou Island, rocks, evidently the north coast. So! The foghorn evidently wasn't working. That coulda' been – it <u>was</u> a near thing.

We slowly motored in a westerly direction until we sighted the Keweenaw Peninsula, then slowly "felt" our way along the northern coastline to Copper Harbor. By the time we arrived at Copper Harbor it was dark.

Entering Copper Harbor required aligning two "range" lights, one ashore and one on a buoy floating at the harbor entrance. When these lights lined up, we could, by keeping them in line, safely enter the harbor between rocks and reefs. Fortunately the fog had lifted sufficiently to see the lights.

Once ashore, nothing seemed as bad as it had been. Clarence's color improved and we soon had a rousing good supper.

In the morning we re-evaluated our plan to sail on to Isle Royal deciding instead to return the way we had come until we had entered Keweenaw Bay then continue southwest to the Portage Canal and up the canal to Houghton/Hancock.

We had to buck a little weather rounding the Keweenaw Peninsula but were soon cruising smoothly and easily toward the Portage Canal entry.

Enroute we discovered we had taken a little water up forward in the sleeping area and some of the bedding had gotten wet. We managed to get the bedding up on deck and spread it out in the sunshine on the forward deck. By the time we had accomplished this we were approaching the canal.

Everyone took a break after the exertion and Clarence had the coffee hot and ready. Mike Dooley climbed up on the foredeck and relaxed on the partially dried bedding. The weather was so fair and the sun so pleasant that Mike stripped to his shorts, lay down, and relaxed.

The steady drone of the boat's engine, the warm sun, the calm sea especially after entering the Portage Canal soon had Mike fast asleep.

Back in those days a touring company used to

run Great Lakes Cruises in a pair of large multi-deck cruising ships, the "North American" and the "South American."

As we were motoring up the canal, the "North American" also entered the canal and rapidly overhauled us. They chose to throttle back and follow us to their berth alongside the canal in Houghton.

The arrival of these cruise ships in Houghton was a big event. Flags and bunting decorations were everywhere. The mayor was there along with the local high school band waiting for the ship, the ship directly behind the Sandra – with Mike Dooley asleep in his shorts on the foredeck.

Flags waved. The band struck up. The "North American" sounded her whistle. The Sandra was just passing the reviewing stand about 40 or 50 feet off shore – and Mike woke up!

Did he panic? Did he scramble for his pants? Did he try to dive below through the open hatchway? He did none of these things.

Rising to his full height (in his shorts, of course) he grandly waved to the assembled throng, bowed to the mayor – who returned his salute – and continued waving to the enthusiastic crowd until we passed from the area. Mike was the star of the show.

Later that evening, after securing the "Sandra" at a berth, we walked up the hill to downtown Hancock. There was a bar and dining facility there – The "Eagle" or something like that – where we had a drink or two and an excellent meal. Mike's fame had spread and, when it was discovered that there was a celebrity in their midst, several complimentary drinks were sent to the table.

The trip from Houghton/Hancock back to Marquette was uneventful. Mike graciously allowed that we wouldn't have to call him "sir" - unless we were ashore and there were strangers around. Werner just shook his head and threatened to "jump ship," hitchhike home to Marquette.

These were good ole' boys and the way they chose to live their lives. I was privileged to have been a part of it.

"Hooooonk!" The foghorn continued its measured signal. I remember snuggling a little deeper in my bunk. Memories drifting gently through my mind, memories brought on by the sound of the foghorn. "Hooooonk!" I like the sound of that old foghorn. It's an old friend.

♎

ARE YOU THE FELLA . . .

I'm gonna try to share something with you here. I don't know if you'd call it a personal thing but the doggone papers and the television are so hyper with news of wars and beatings and cheatings that I thought I'd try to plug in something to make you smile, maybe reminisce pleasantly in your easy chair. This is "everyday life" at its happiest and best.

The other day I got an e-mail. You know, one of those electronic letters you get on the computer. It started out, "Are you the Ben Mukkala that was stationed down in Fort Worth back in 1952 when . . ." and it went on describing Air Force life at Fort Worth. It was signed Richard T. Nicolls, M.D. 1952! Boy! That was a long time ago but I was there and I was the guy he was asking about. By way of telling him I was that fella I sent back a message I felt he should be able to identify with. "If you're the guy I danced with . . ." Now before you all get the wrong idea, I'd better start that story from the beginning.

Back in 1952 three of us, young Air Force guys, Richard "Nick" Nicolls from San Bernadino, California, Donald McFadden from up around Boston, Massachusetts, and myself, from Michigan, were all stationed at Carswell Air Force Base. The evening we're discussing we all had dates with three lovely young ladies, friends of one another, in Fort Worth. The evening was going nicely with drinks and dinner and drinks and dancing and, well – and Nick might argue with me here – Nick had dipped into the barrel of "Old Cordwood" maybe a little too deep. His date was a bit upset with his making merry. Shucks, we had all been toasting one another in a rather unrestricted fashion. Anyway his date in particular was concerned with his driving, perturbed with the way the evening was proceeding – in short she was PO'd.

We had stopped at a little watering hole with a small dance floor on the second floor, for whoever might be familiar with Fort Worth, it was out along Camp Bowie Boulevard on the west side of town. The mood of the group had become reserved. Nick's date was downright chilly.

We had stopped, parked, gone upstairs and found a table. We ordered drinks and settled in. It was one of those somewhat secluded spots and on this night it wasn't overly crowded. In an attempt to lighten the atmosphere and bring a little gaiety to the proceedings – I guess that's what he had in mind – Nick rose in a most gentlemanly manner and asked his date to dance. Not a good move under the circumstances. His date raised her head, poked out her pretty little chin and replied with a distinct and definite "No!" Taken a bit aback but not a bit discouraged Nick flamboyantly turned to my date and repeated his request. My young lady squirmed a little uncomfortably, shot a surreptitious glance at her companions, looked down at her drink and also replied "No, thank you" but in a more subdued tone. Still not recognizing the futility of his mission or just being bull-headed, Nick plowed on determined to "live in fame or go down in flames." He turned to Don's date and again repeated his offer. Same response. There he was, standing beside the dance floor – alone. You guys all know what that's like. It was obvious by now to the whole establishment that he was making his pitch to these young ladies and that he was striking out.

I strongly suspect that from the age of about three girls are aware that they have the capability of crushing the confidence, the self-image, the joie de vivre, the ego of any young fella. Our would be Don Juan may boldly walk across a dance floor in a crowded bistro to ask the lady of his choice to dance. There are various ways she can refuse but that brief, sharp one syllable response, "No," can crush him to powder. For our would-be great lover it may have been a short stroll across the floor with his request. After that curt refusal it is always a long and painful journey back across a hostile desert with everyone watching – and knowing. Every step of the way he's trying to invent a face saving story to tell his friends. This was the situation that was rapidly becoming clear to Nick's otherwise confident composure – or maybe not.

With nowhere to hide and not wanting to face that "long walk" back around the (little) table, he turned to me. "Would you care to dance?" he asked in his most eloquent manner.

"Why, certainly," I replied graciously. And we did.

That is to say we began dancing – I don't remember who was leading. Our young ladies went into shock reacting as if we had suggested that their mommas and poppas hadn't known one another very well. Don McFadden just leaned back and guffawed startling the whole establishment.

Our sudden fame gained us some notoriety among the patrons of the place and was a little too much for management to accept. This incident, you must remember, was occurring before the days of "Gay Rights" and "don't ask, don't tell." The bouncer, a big burly guy who hangs out near the end of the bar – all places of this sort have one, walked out on the dance floor and "made us an offer we couldn't refuse." He suggested to Nick and I that maybe we should leave.

McFadden was laughing so hard he could hardly walk down the stairs. The girls, well, to say they were flustered is an understatement. I overheard a tense under-the-breath comment of one to another, "Everyone was looking at us!" Nick and I were upset too. We hadn't gotten to finish our dance.

Needless to say there was no "parking and sparking" after that little episode. Matter of fact I don't believe we ever saw those girls again. Ah, well, there were a lot of pretty girls in Fort Worth. And, what the heck, we were Air Force men - braving the wild blue yonder - keeping the world safe – "Peace was our Profession," all that sort of thing. One minor disappointment but none of us even got out of step – one for all and all for one – "and all that jazz."

Anyway that's what that message, sent "in the dark," lit up in my memory. There were many more memories and I'm sure Nick and I will talk them over. I imagine it will be on the e-mail as he's out in the state of Washington while I'm in Michigan. We both wondered about Don McFadden – I think it was Sewickley, or maybe it was Newton? Massachusetts he was from – and whether we'd ever cross paths with him again.

We were, all three, Corporals or Buck Sergeants back then. I went on to become a pilot and complete twenty years in the Air Force. Nick got out at the end of his hitch, used the GI Bill and became a doctor. He's retired now, as I am, out in Washington State. Don McFadden? Neither Nick nor I have heard from him. From what I remember of Don, he may be in jail somewhere. If you're out there, buddy, give us a holler.

Well that's a tale from the misty past. That's life. I hope you enjoyed reading about it half as much as I did living it. And it is a respite from the stories of shootings and rapes and "wars and rumors of wars."

Ω

Life is Not a Destination

REACH FOR THE SKY

I have spent a good bit of my life flying airplanes and associating with folks who build, maintain and fly airplanes. People in service to their fellow man are not doing it for fame and glory. They have a need to search for, to explore, to try something new. They are people "Who know the great enthusiasm, the great devotion, who spends themselves in a worthy cause." Just as in the military service, with which I am also familiar, the recognition, the medals and the adulation go to a few. There are many overlooked whose contributions were even greater.

Kick back, prop your boots on a footrest and let's log a little flyin' time.

Life is Not a Destination

HIGH FLIGHT

Oh! I have slipped the surly bonds of Earth
And danced the skies on laughter-silvered wings;
Sunward I've climbed, and joined the tumbling mirth
Of sun-split clouds, — and done a hundred things
You have not dreamed of — wheeled and soared
and swung
High in the sunlit silence. Hov'ring there,
I've chased the shouting wind along, and flung
My eager craft through footless halls of air. . . .

Up, up the long, delirious burning blue
I've topped the wind-swept heights with easy grace
Where never lark, or ever eagle flew —
And, while with silent, lifting mind I've trod
The high untrespassed sanctity of space,
Put out my hand, and touched the face of God.

— *John Gillespie Magee, Jr*

For aviators – and anyone else interested in aviation – December 17th holds a special significance. On that date in 1903 at Kitty Hawk, North Carolina, Orville and Wilbur Wright launched the world up, up and away into the age of aviation. A National Memorial commemorating their achievement stands on that site today.

Imagine that, if you would, two bicycle repairmen rechecking calculations – those they could calculate, guessing at or estimating those they couldn't - manhandling a tethered glider, attempting to measure the lift and drag with hand-held spring-loaded scales. They were preparing to attempt something that risked their very lives. They would "boldly go where no man has gone before." They were going to try to fly!

An Englishman may be compelled to add an aside here - that it was a fellow named George Cagley, in 1853, that designed and flew a glider. It was a glider because it had no means of propulsion. There weren't any engines suitable for an aircraft back in those days. Mr. Cagley had a plan for an engine though. It was to be powered by gunpowder. Somehow the whole idea sort of "blew up." (A little "har, har" chuckle is appropriate here.) And in truth it was Mr. Cagley's coachman who rode the glider on its maiden flight. But that was the way things were done in Jolly Old England in those days. "I say, old boy. Good show and all that."

Down in Brazil the name was Alberto Santos Dumont, he is forever attached to flight. He was "first," at least as far as flying down in Brazil is concerned. Mr. Santos was a dashing and good-looking fellow who dazzled the crowds and charmed the ladies and secured himself a position in Brazilian legend. Don't say this openly to Brazilians but have you ever noticed that all we flyers are "good-looking fellows who dazzle the crowds and charm the ladies?" So that accomplishment of Alberto Santos Dumont is no big deal. Oh, and I must not forget that the ladies who have made aviation a sorority are certainly able to hold up their end of the wing tip also.

In New Zealand the aviation pioneer's name that comes to the fore is Richard Pearse. The date of his flight is cited as March 31, 1903. That's <u>March 1903,</u> almost a year before Orville and Wilbur flew down at Kitty Hawk. Hmmmm! That's something to think about.

And the French have Bleriot who contributed knowledge and publicity to aviation endeavors and the (flying) crossing of the English Channel.

And none of us should overlook Icarus of Greek legend, the son of Daedalus. Daedalus designed and constructed wings of wax and feathers. The father's invention enabled the two of them to escape the prison to which the King had sentenced them. Daedalus flew all the way to Naples and escaped. Icarus, dazzled and excited by the realm of flight, disregarded his father's warning and flew too close to the sun. The sun melted the wax holding the feathers and Icarus fell from the sky. This made him the first brash young airman to bust his – err, ahem – who "bought the farm" as a result of disregarding the learned council of older and wiser heads. Truth be told, many of today's young flyers suffer from the same malady – and too many experience the same result.

After the celebration and the commemorating have passed one might pause in a quiet moment to remember those others – all those others. Orville and Wilbur and those we have lightly mentioned climbed to their lofty positions on the backs and shoulders of many who went before, who blazed the path. There are few laurels for those who fail but they, too, made contributions. They showed the ways that wouldn't work and often paid for that knowledge with their lives. In their memory we recall the words of President Theodore Roosevelt:

"It is not the critic who counts; not the man who points out how the strong man stumbles, or where the doer of deeds could have done them better. The credit belongs to the man who is actually in the arena, whose face is marred by dust and sweat and blood, who strives valiantly; who errs and comes short again and again. Who knows the great enthusiasm, the great devotion, who spends himself in a worthy cause. Who at the best knows in the end the triumph of high achievement and who at the worst, if he fails, at least he fails while daring greatly so that his place shall never be with those cold and timid souls who know neither victory nor defeat."

A moment of silence if you will – and a salute – to all our "band of brothers" – and sisters - who have blazed the trail to the stars, "put out their hands, and touched the face of God."

℧

"Aviation,
to an even greater extent than the sea,
is terribly unforgiving of any
carelessness, incapacity or neglect."

Life is Not a Destination

Winter

"Have you ever been out in the great alone
when the moon is bright and clear?
And the icy mountains hem you in
With a silence you 'most could hear?"

Robert W. Service

Life is Not a Destination

A WALK IN THE WINTER WOODS AT NIGHT

Walking in the woods in the dark is a good way to break your leg - or worse - unless there's a bright moon. Even then, stumbling through the woods in the dark is - is - well it's a kind of adventure. I did hike through the woods to camp one summer night. My pickup truck had broken down on the trail. The left front wheel suspension knuckle came - well - that's another story for another time. There was no moon that night but the stars were bright - bright enough that I could stay on the trail if I used a lot of imagination. You kind of had to look up, through the trees overhead, to see if you could tell which way the trail went. Coming out of a little dip where the road crossed a creek - I was feeling my way along in the dark - a partridge suddenly "exploded!" right under my feet! My eyes flew open wide enough that I should have been able to see as well as any owl. Every hair I had - and I don't have many - turned white, I believe, right then. In winter a walk in the woods is different.

My teenage son was visiting for Christmas one year. He lives with his mother in Texas but was up for the holidays. We had snowshoed the couple miles to this little cabin I have up on the Yellow Dog River in Upper Michigan. We got there in the early afternoon, lit the fires, and got the bunks made. The sun sets early in winter and, this night, a beautiful full moon rose. It was a brilliant, icy white in a clear velvet blue sky. The wooded hills stood out as plain as daylight. I have to pause here to confess that I had planned ahead for this. I wanted the boy to have some good memories of his dad and his dad's country and lifestyle. I couldn't have asked for a better evening than this one.

I suggested we hike down to the river and "eat out" - the way we do it up here in the woods where we don't have a fast-food place on every corner. I packed a lunch. We strapped on our snowshoes, and struck off down the trail. It was a bit dark at first but, as our eyes adapted, the winter woods emerged in silent splendor. The full moon reflected blue-white off the snow. Shadows of trees and bare branches etched outlines in ebony on the white snow. The silence was absolute. Our breath made small white clouds in the frigid air.

Slow and easy is the way to go. Too much effort generates perspiration that quickly invites the cold. I tried to tailor the pace to my son's stride stopping frequently just to look around. After a half mile or so the sound of the river grew louder. We had sandwiches and a thermos of hot chocolate in our pack. Lunch would be on the riverbank. Stomping down a snow area behind a drift on the riverbank, we took off our snowshoes, broke up some dead branches, and laid a bed for a campfire. A few pine boughs to sit on and our lunch-camp was made. We toasted sandwiches on forked sticks over the fire. A frozen tree somewhere in the forest split with a sound like a rifle shot. It was cold.

With a warm lunch and hot chocolate in our bellies, Benny and I were enjoying what the books call "quality time." The beauty of the surroundings was awesome. The river chuckled and murmured in the background.

Stars were bright as diamonds - so close you felt you could touch them. At times like this, silence speaks louder than words.

Our lunch camp was on a river bend due south of the cabin - a little over a quarter of a mile away. (This was planned also.) As we stared at the sky I pointed out the star-cluster called Ursa Major, the great bear. It makes up the big dipper. Benny recognized the big dipper.

"Son, the two stars that make up the lip of the dipper - see them? - line them up and extend the line about five times the distance between them. You'll come to another bright star. Do you see it?" He did. "Do you see how bright it is? How easy it is to identify? To find it?" Again he nods in the affirmative. "Well, Benny, that star is Polaris, the North Star. Whenever you locate that star, you'll know that that direction is north. It happens that our cabin is straight north from here. You can't see it. It's too far away and it's behind a hill but, if you follow that star, it'll lead you back to camp."

We sat silently staring at the stars in the flickering firelight.

"Here's what I'd like you to do. We'll break camp - put out the fire - and, using the North Star, you lead us back to camp."

There's a pause as he considered this.

"I'll be right there with you. Wherever you lead I'll be right there. If you have any questions, just ask. You lead and I'll follow. We'll go back to camp."

We packed and put on our snowshoes. A little snow

took care of putting out the fire. It took a few minutes for our eyes, constricted by the firelight, to dilate once more. "Night vision," they call it. Benny picked out the North Star, selected a path, and led the way. He detoured here and there to avoid heavy brush or deadfalls. He checked his direction frequently, checking the North Star.

Before we left the cabin I had lit a kerosene "hurricane lamp" and placed it in the kitchen window on the south side of the cabin.

We snowshoed through a stand of naked maple trees and struggled up a rather steep hill all the while taking it slow and easy. The going was easier across the flat beyond. Only the swish swish of our snowshoes broke the silence. We breasted a small ridgeline and there, just ahead, that hurricane lamp glowed in the cabin window. The soft lantern light shown through the trees reflecting golden on the white blanket of snow. It was beautiful.

Back inside the warm cabin we took off our heavy clothing and got comfortable. A fresh stick of wood rejuvenated the flickering flames in the fireplace. Neither of us spoke much. There didn't seem to be a need. We stared into the flickering flames and glowing coals of the fire - fire that hasn't changed since an ancient cave man first came upon a lightning-struck tree. I wonder what he might have thought? Outside black outlines of naked trees slowly stalked across the white snow. The moon moved toward the western horizon. Eyelids grew heavy. Warm bunks beckoned.

It had been a good day. There'd be bacon and eggs

and fried potatoes in the morning. The adventure would start anew. But, for tonight, it doesn't get any better than this. When he's grown, I hope he remembers these times we had together. They're called memories.

KEEP LOOKIN' UP

Had lunch the other day with some folks who live in a little Senior Citizen's community on the edge of Marquette in Michigan's Upper Peninsula. It's a beautiful location called Lost Creek. It's not on the map. It's just on the edge of Marquette. There were about thirty or so people who gathered for a prepared lunch this day. The Senior Citizens Center in Marquette arranges lunch.

One of the most noticeable features of the gathering was the positive upbeat attitude of everyone there. These were older folks. There was laughter, joking and a good mood everywhere.

I guess the stresses and strains of day-to-day living tend to keep younger people up-tight and operating "right on the edge." That's a shame. They seem to have forgotten or maybe they never knew the secret of avoiding heartburn and headaches. The Indians would say they don't yet know where the center of the earth is.

The gathering begins with the little daily greetings: "Hi! How are you?" "How's it goin'?" And you want to remember what, I think it was President Harry Truman who said, "Those are just greetings. No one but your doctor really wants an answer." A person is expected to reply in the same context. It would be a real surprise if someone paused and said, "Well, I've got this pain – right down here – you know? And I have to get up four or five times every night to . . ." No, you don't answer that way. You just smile back and say "Fine!" These are simply greetings, the day-to-day niceties that are the lubricant to social interaction. If somebody is having a bad day and tends to complain, they're tolerated for a day – or two. If it continues that person is apt to find him (or her) self eating alone.

When you were a kid your parents told you about these things. This is how you get along with others. Say "please" and "thank you." Show respect for the rights and the feelings of others. "That's Mary's toy." "Share with each other." "Don't say mean things." "Play nice together."

As a child gets older and goes out into the world those things their folks told them shouldn't be forgotten. Unfortunately the golden rule often becomes, "Do unto others as you think they might to do unto you – and do it first!" Is that because they have forgotten what their parents told them? Or is it because what they saw their parents doing was much louder? Children aren't as naive as adults would like to believe. They learn much more from what they see grownups do than by what they hear them say – and that can cancel out anything you might say in the future too. The thunder of actions drowns out the whispers of speech. These are what shape a child's character. Bend the twig and that's how the tree will grow.

Another snare that entraps a child – and some adults
- is when they try to make life easier by telling a lie. A lie
will probably work once - or twice. It may work several
times but once it's exposed a delicate thread called trust
has been broken. Being a "little" dishonest is like being
a "little" pregnant. In both cases either you are or you
aren't. Honesty is a critical part of that much-faceted
quality called character. Older people seem more aware
of these things.

Kids quickly learn that life's a competition. They
should learn to compete honestly. The world will reward
a person in accordance with what they are able to do,
how well they are able to do it and how difficult it is
to replace them. An important ingredient of success
is strength of character, self-preparation and dedicated
effort. Some believe they elevate themselves by tearing
down others. They're exposing a weakness in their
character. A person reveals what they are in the way they
treat others, particularly others who are at the moment
subordinate to them.

It's not until a person gets older that they realize that
parenting is the most critical occupation in the world. A
failure to prepare children, particularly pre-school age
children, can create the most terrifying of all "Weapons
of Mass Destruction." Parenting shapes the future.
Teach those kids by your example. It's only the weak
that are critical, mean, arrogant and cruel. Gentleness,
kindness, consideration comes only from people who

have confidence and who like themselves; it's to be expected only from the strong.

You might pass on to your kids what an army general once told his troops: "He who feels and hence manifests disrespect toward others cannot fail to excite a strong resentment and disrespect toward themselves." Tell them in your own words, of course. Disrespect, like a lie, is a no-win situation. Why is it we must grow old to realize these things? "So soon old, so late smart?"

Two character descriptions come to mind: "If (so and so) said it, you can take it to the bank!" "Well, he may be a 'good ole boy' but keep him in front of you." These are metaphors of course but you know what they're saying. And there always seem to be those few who are just genuine unadulterated SOBs. They are their own worst enemies and are often beyond the time and trouble to attempt to recover them. Just avoid them.

The folks at Lost Creek know these things. They know the original golden rule is still the best way to go. They remember the lessons they learned as children. Say "please" and "thank you." Share. Don't say mean things and hurt people. Respect each other. It's not material things that make a person wealthy but the number of people who are glad you touched their lives.

It's called Character. And I guess you could say Lost Creek is full of characters.

♎

LOOK FOR THE SUNSHINE

Winter in our north country is closely associated with snow and cold; short hours of daylight and gray overcast skies. The particular year I mention here the temperature has only been moderately chilly and the anticipated heavy snow seems to be passing us in favor of the east coast. We have had our share of overcast skies however. It's a normal part of the season. The lack of snow and warmer than usual temperatures has put a crimp in snowmobiling, slowed up the skiers and left local business people with dust gathering on their cash registers. The lack of recreational visitors is depressing but the short hours of daylight and gray overcast skies are also a covert depressant. To know the problem is half of the solution.

The only answer to the snowmobile/ski problem is lower temperatures and more snow. Winter resort owners, those of Scandinavian persuasion and a few converts who have become "true believers," will have been conducting "Heikke Lunta" snow dances already. Let's move on from the commercial aspect of the weather and talk a little about this other depressant, the overcast skies and short hours of daylight.

There are "sunshine lamps" advertised in newspapers, magazines and on television. Maybe they help, I don't know. I have spoken to people who swear by them. Back when I was in the service, the United States Air Force, when the troops were depressed the powers that be would arrange some entertainment. Maybe it was a party or a visiting troop of entertainers or maybe just some (hopefully) charismatic guy from higher headquarters to tell us what a great job we were doing, what a great bunch of people we were. It usually worked to some degree but it was referred to by the troops as "the sunshine pump" as in "They're sending in the sunshine pump to pump us up." Maybe the sunshine lamp works just as well. The important thing in both instances is that the problem has been recognized. That in itself is a major accomplishment.

I regularly have coffee and/or breakfast with different groups of "good ole boys" each week. The differences between individuals in those groups are easily recognized. Since I'm 75 years old myself you're safe in assuming the "good ole boys" are not teenagers. These are folks who have traveled life's highway for a few miles already and it hasn't all been on paved roads. Unfortunately some of the wives/husbands have died. The survivors are all too often living alone. Their children (those who have had children) have long since left the nest and are busy raising families of their own. Some of the kids will check on their elderly parent regularly – or not so regularly. Many are so occupied with the trials and travails of their own lives and children that the old folks have dropped to a lower priority. The parents understand remembering the way it was for them at that age and don't complain. That's the way it is.

And at this stage the younger generation feels they are immortal and have little conception of growing old. Middle age is hyper involved with trying to control that younger generation, earning a living and paying the bills. Keeping all three of those balls in the air simultaneously doesn't leave much time for philosophizing about mortality. Recognition of that mortality might temper their attitude toward "old geezers." Showing up for one of our breakfasts and discovering that one of our number isn't there – and isn't going to be there - anymore - ever is a fact of life. Growing old is not for sissies.

Now comes Mukkala's Theorem as applied to enjoying and extending those years we still have. It ties in with the sun lamp and the sunshine pump thing. If a person believes that a treatment or potion or exercise or pill will cure their ills, it probably will. But I also believe there is more "health" generated by a person's mental attitude than in all the pill bottles on all the pharmacy's shelves in the world. This idea is not something I picked up in church or from "sniffin' glue." This idea is supported by medically supervised and independently controlled tests. Medical specialists assemble a group of patients suffering from some ailment. They will all be given what appears (to them) to be a treatment – pill, potion or activity – to "cure" the problem. Some will receive a specifically designed – whatever it might be – developed and believed to have the ability to cure or improve the patient's health. Others will be given what's called a "placebo" - a "sugar pill" - a treatment that should have no recognizable benefit. To make it what they call a truly "blind" study, many of the medical technicians administrating the test don't know who is getting the genuine treatment and who is receiving the placebo either. The patients taking part in the test, of course, have no knowledge of who is getting what.

The perfect solution from a medical point of view would be when all patients receiving the "real" medicine improve or are cured while those receiving the placebo show a worsening or no change. If the comparison does not come out perfect, at least the number of actually treated patients should have a much higher percentage of "cure" than the "blind" group.

In many tests those receiving the real medicine showed better results as was expected – but not in all cases. What's even more noteworthy to you and I is that so many receiving placebos also showed marked improvement – more than could be accounted for by random chance. This occurrence is not attributed to voodoo witchcraft but to the fact that your mind has a great deal of control over the other organs of your body. You have the ability to internally generate antibodies and enzymes and all sorts of goodies that are capable of curing and or maintaining your health. That built-in ability and the power of belief is probably what makes voodoo and witchdoctor treatments work too. You've gotta believe in yourself!

Now comes the first corollary to Mukkala's Theorem – I guess I can call it that? A fella named Norman Cousins was once suffering from a painful illness related to rheumatism and arthritis. After exhaustive testing and examination it was determined there didn't seem to be an effective treatment. He was hurtin' and there was nothing those folks in the white coats could do for him. To keep the story short and to the point, he discovered that when he could laugh he could also alleviate the pain. He followed up on this discovery. He would watch movies, comedies, slapstick humor – Abbott and Costello, the Marx brothers, Bugs Bunny cartoons, anything that gave him a laugh. He even established a graph of the relationship between the amount and depth of his laughter and the duration of his pain relief. He wrote a book about it; "Anatomy of an Illness."

So, comes the first corollary to Mukkala's Theorem. It's plagiarized from Mr. Normal Cousins: laughter can brighten the skies, improve the digestion, and make you a better and happier person. You may even come to like yourself. Liking yourself is not so easy as you might first assume.

I'm going to throw in a quotation here. It's from John Steinbeck, a rather famous journalist with a broad knowledge of the human condition. He's the fella who wrote "The Grapes of Wrath." If you haven't read The Grapes of Wrath or seen it as a movie, it's the story of a poor family helping each other and surviving during the Great Depression. It's a powerful statement about the human spirit. I recommend it and I think it supports my Theorem and Corollary:

"Most people do not like themselves at all. They distrust themselves, put on masks and pomposities. They quarrel and boast and pretend and are jealous because they do not like themselves. . . .If we could learn to like ourselves even a little, maybe our cruelties and anger might melt away. Maybe we would not have to hurt one another just to keep our ego chins above water."

In your everyday living get together with other people for coffee, for breakfast, for lunch, for whatever reason. If you know of someone who isn't able to get there themselves include them, arrange to pick them up

– or have someone else do it - and make him or her a member of your group.

Here's another little secret for a happy life. It's not money that brings happiness. It's what we do to and for one another.

A Behavior Psychologist named Abraham Maslow called it "self-actualization." It could also be called a feeling of having accomplished something of importance. What it's called is not important. It's what you do, the appreciation you receive, and even without appreciation the pleasure you feel at having done a worthwhile thing. This is what allows you to like yourself.

One of the practices of any group you're associated with should be to emphasize positive things. Everybody knows there are crooked politicians, shyster lawyers, and bad weather. They're what make the headlines in newspapers and are the lead story on the television news. But there are other politicians, lawyers, and men and women working hard to make our society greater and better than it is. And there are many days when the sun is shining but we're so busy grubbing in the ditch we've dug in our daily lives that we don't look up and see it. Good things are happening all around. Talk about them too.

Now don't rush out and fire your doctor but know that the more you enjoy, the more you laugh, the more you emphasize the positive the better you're going to feel. And the better you feel the longer you'll live to go on laughing and enjoying.

I'll bet your doctor will tell you that same thing – but of course he charges more than I do.

♎

"Laugh and the world laughs with you.

Cry and you cry alone."

ENTERTAINING WINTER NEIGHBORS

As the long and dreary days of winter drag by some of us begin to feel trapped in our houses. One day is just like the day before. There seems to be no end in sight. Trying to get out for a walk or a short drive can become more of an adventure than was intended especially if freezing rain has coated the highways, the walkways, and is working at the tip of your nose. Here's a suggestion that can create a diversion and at times hilarious entertainment. Set up an outside feeding station for birds or squirrels or anything that might stop by. It doesn't have to be elaborate. Anything from bread crumbs scattered on the porch to elaborate sheltered feeders on a "critter-proof" pole. And if the squirrels get into the bird feeder, so what? The squirrel's gotta eat too.

Dorothy discovered a couple of screw-on attachments for those large (they're bigger than quart size) plastic pop bottles. It comes with an easily attachable wire hanger. You punch a couple small holes in the pop bottle through which the hanger wire attaches. Fill the bottle with sunflower seeds, or millet and hang it on a tree branch or the eave of the house – whatever. It'll bring chickadees to beat the band. We also have a wire suet cage hanging from an eave. Woodpeckers really like that. That suet – fat – can be bought for little or nothing from your local meat market. When the temperature drives the thermometer down those little birds need to burn that fat to keep warm and survive.

A shelf attached to a tree trunk – just a vertical board with another shorter board attached with screws at a 90-degree angle is all you'll need. It's not going to have to hold much weight and can also be relatively short – 6 inches or so. Then run a longer screw through the bottom of the shelf so as to protrude an inch or so. Just take an ear of corn (feed corn from an outdoor feed store) and screw it down on that protruding screw. (See the picture at the head of this story.)

The squirrels like to get lunch there. We have chickadees, nuthatches, woodpeckers, squirrels, crows, doves; we even had a fox come by one day. By placing these feeders where they can be easily seen from the kitchen table or your easy chair or someplace where you spend time. That way watching the feeders isn't the only thing you do and you won't become impatient waiting for your dinner guests.

The birds will set up their own schedule based upon - I don't know - phases of the moon, I guess. The crows are super cautious when they approach. The seed that falls on the ground and the occasional chunk of suet we toss down there seems to attract them. That suet is what brought the fox, I believe, but that's another story.

If you try to plan to watch by your schedule you're in for frustration. Don't "plan." Just let it happen. As things occur, birds feeding, squirrels coming, whatever, they'll establish a schedule. It may become as regular as a bus schedule - or not - but it'll be their schedule, not yours.

The chickadees flit in, look quickly around, select a seed, and fly to a branch. They'll hold it on the branch with their foot and break it open by striking it with their beak. Sometime they'll drop it. Oh, well, go back for another. Those dropped seeds will attract other ground feeding birds. Crows, too.

The nuthatches will land on the bird feeder but they'll also light on the tree trunk. Right side up, up side down, it makes no difference to them. They, like the chickadees, will dig under the bark and in the tiny crevasses for the eggs and tiny bugs that are there.

Crows will approach in a round-about manner, checking the area for danger. You may get to watch them awhile before they ever come to the feed - seeds or bread or suet or anything - on the ground. If there are several of them they'll probably have at least one posted as a lookout. I often wondered how they decide who gets guard duty.

Squirrels come by - at their leisure, of course. There are a couple red squirrels and at least one gray squirrel. The gray is warier than the red squirrels. The red squirrel is the "loud mouth." They chatter and scold and twitch their tails, If the corn-cob feeder is empty they sometime perch on the porch railing near the kitchen sliding glass door, look in at me drinking coffee, and raise h—l 'til I replace the corn cob.

We even had a flying squirrel come by. They're a nocturnal creature and are very shy. It was one of those things where I saw a movement outside near a feeder. When I looked - nothing seemed to be there. Was it my imagination? There's nothing - wait - wait - motionless and looking back from large dark liquid eyes, motionless, was the squirrel. I just backed slowly away and let him eat.

You've got to have a few trees around to have squirrels - not many, but a few. Birds seem to come regardless of the surroundings. It doesn't take much to attract these outdoor neighbors and they'll give you hours of entertainment. What the heck. It's winter, the TV's not that great, and you're not doing anything else anyway. Give it a shot!

By the way, did you know that the name, "squirrel"

comes from two Greek words, "skia" meaning shade, and "oura" meaning tail. So, putting those two together, "squirrel" means "he who sits in the shadow of his own tail." One of life's nagging questions I'm sure you have been losing sleep over. It's also one of those things you can casually mention at a party when conversation lags.

♎

"He liveth best who loveth best
Both man and bird and beast.
He liveth best who loveth best
All things both great and small
For the dear God who loveth us
He made and loveth – all."

Samuel Coleridge

Life is Not a Destination

Spring

LIFE GOES ON

He stands alone, a Canadian goose on an old log raft floating in our bayou. At first glance it looks like there might be a problem, that that goose is disabled, crippled. His head is tucked under his wing and he's only standing on one leg. A couple ducks paddle by but he pays no attention. Any unusual movement or sound, anything out of tune with his environment elicits an immediate response. That's what happened when I stepped out on the porch. He quickly raises his head. That other leg magically appeared. It's now apparent that the first impression was wrong. He is immediately awake, alert and prepared for fight or flight. Creatures in the natural world are used to these conditions. They're matter-offactly living on the edge of disaster every day. And every day their world tests the difference between the quick and the dead.

This time of year that goose I'm watching is probably the gander, the male. The goose, the female will be hidden somewhere close by incubating a clutch of eggs. The nest will be made of dry grass and a few feathers in which she will have laid three to six eggs. She would be about half way through their incubation period of 25 or 30 days. Once they hatch the goslings will immediately be led out to feed on marsh grass, green shoots and, I hope, a little of the whole corn I toss to them every day.

The gander's duty is to guard the nesting area and share in the care and feeding when the goslings hatch. That gander will not hesitate to attack whatever threatens his mate or the nest. You may feel that doesn't apply to you and I. You'd better think again. A gander can weigh up to eighteen pounds. Its wings can be eight feet across and very muscular. When migrating, geese are capable of sustained flights of up to sixteen hours non-stop. With a favorable tail wind they can manage speeds of up to 70 miles per hour. If you're inclined to casually search for the nest keep that physical condition in mind and that the gander has got the guts, the "sisu" to take you on. In a fight in nature, there are no gentlemanly rules. You might also remember the adage, "It's not the size of the (goose) in the fight but the size of the fight in the (goose)." When you get up close, that gander is

---

pretty big.

There's a fella up in Canada you could ask about that. He once lay with a broken leg for two hours waiting for someone to find him. His demise was the result of an encounter with an angry goose. All right, all right, I'll tell you the whole story.

The guy was walking in the woods, minding his own business when he encountered this gander. The bird attacked him. It's assumed there must have been a nest close by. The fella broke his leg when he fell as he was trying to run away. The bird didn't kick him while he was down or anything. To the gander, the threat had been removed. End of story. There was no feeling of a need for revenge. That's a trait worth noting among animals. They don't get involved with the psychological hang-ups humans suffer from. If a threat arises, they contend with it. When the threat is eliminated they move on. We may call them "dumb animals" but it's interesting that we're the ones going to psychiatrists. Shouldn't we be learning something from that?

I've been watching that gander and his mate on and off for a month or so now, ever since they returned to our bayou. I say returned because I believe they've been here before. They flew in and began looking the area over, shopping for a nesting site before the ice was full gone. Other geese stopped by but these two left no doubt as to who had seniority in this area. With their necks extended they let out a warning squawk and were after them like a B-52 jet bomber. I haven't seen actual physical encounters but the welcome mat is most definitely not out. The uninvited guests don't seem inclined to argue.

There's a lot to admire about geese. A pair will mate for life and they may live for up to 24 years. It's only when death do them part that the surviving goose will seek another mate.

I heard a story of a gander that stayed with his injured mate all winter rather than migrating south. I'm sure it helped that a farmer in whose pond they were living provided feed. There was also an old shed nearby that afforded them shelter. Do you wonder why that farmer did that? I'd bet you he might be a little embarrassed if you asked him. I feel I understand why and therefore I admire him for it. It's what I would have done too.

On average those geese are probably, in their social order, healthier and better adjusted than most of us. Their lifestyle, honesty, fidelity and their lack of inhibition might have something to do with it. They may indiscriminately poop everywhere – but never on each other. That's a whole 'nother thought, isn't it? There's a lot to admire about a goose.

Ω

WHERE THERE IS NO PATH

There's a small cabin on ten acres of land between Marquette and Big Bay in Michigan's Upper Peninsula. The Yellow Dog River wanders through the woods just a quarter of a mile away. The next nearest neighbor is about two and a half miles farther along on an old, abandoned logging road. There are no highways, no power lines, no telephones, no running water (except in a small creek near the door), and no stress. A few deer occasionally stop by evenings on their way to wherever.

A couple of woodchucks carried on a courtship under the woodshed for a few days, then chased each other off into the aspens just east of the cabin. Field mice were in evidence even though foodstuffs were secured in cans or inside metal cupboards. Everybody has got to be somewhere and that's where everybody was.

A few patches of snow were still hiding in the shaded spots but the buds were popping out on the maples, aspens, and birches. The fiddleheads of emerging ferns were poking up through the dead leaves on the forest floor along with violets, spring beauties, adder's-tongues, and the shy, trailing, arbutus "mayflower."

It was great to be alive. I wandered through the valleys and over the rocks just soaking up the spring sunshine and watching the earth experience the resurrection that happens each spring in these northern climes.

I had discovered a beaver pond about a mile or so west of the camp. It was in a very secluded spot on a small stream, away from trails and roads. A number of brown trout lived there and were hungry enough to bite your finger if you put it in the water. Evidence indicated that not too many people knew where this spot was. I saw no reason for changing that.

The proprietor of the establishment, a large brown beaver, swam casually by, looking me over pretty carefully. He evidently decided that I would be permitted to share the hospitality of his domain.

Worms alternated with small silver spinners soon provided me with three fine brown trout about ten or twelve inches long. (I could have made them bigger, you know—BELIEVE!)

A bit of the ending of the day was spent sitting on the bank watching trout rising to early flies among the lengthening shadows and listening to the gurgle and splash of the water escaping through the sticks of the dam. The old beaver would occasionally pass on an inspection tour of the ramparts.

Heaven is a wonderful place, I am told, but I'm not really anxious to leave here just yet.

Speaking of leaving here, the sun is about to disappear beyond the hills and I had better turn my attention to getting back to the cabin. The early spring chill is beginning to settle through the woods.

I have a pocket compass and decide to take a direct

route to an old skid way that should be a little easier walking with less probability of becoming disoriented in the gathering dusk. I don't have an area map, but I have been roaming through these woods since my father first brought me out here when I was about ten or twelve. That's got to be, gosh, forty years ago.

Let's see. Getting here, I came west from the cabin, through a cut in the rocks, then sort of southwest —a little more westerly - to hit the creek, or, if luck held, run right onto the beaver pond.

That skidding trail I have in mind is a bit north of my southwesterly leg and zigzags in a generally northerly direction joining the main trail before turning east through the rocky ridge. It passes just north of my cabin. If I leave here heading just a little east of north, I should come out on that skidding trail just over a quarter of a mile from here.

The trout are still rising on the pond. Mosquitoes are gathering around me but the bug dope seems to be keeping them from lighting. I'm resigned to their whining flight and their hovering in my face.

I recall a promotional sign I once saw on a housing division near Indianapolis, Indiana, "If you lived in Sunnydale, you'd be home now."

If I had brought my sleeping bag and a pup tent, I'd be "home" now too. Well, I didn't and I'm not. The outlines of things distant are beginning to get a little indistinct. Better get a move on.

The beaver pond is barely out of sight before the

high land gives way to a swampy area with thick alder brush and fallen trees.

I elect to bear east a little more until I am clear of this brush. I'll then correct back to the west to maintain my course. No need to check the compass again. I have just left the pond; it's, let's see, back about there, and I want to head about this way but, instead will angle over toward that pine tree standing alone among the aspen on that ridge. I guess that's what they are. Anyway, that's the way I'm going to go.

Hey! Just what I needed! One foot went down into the muck with a little water over the boot top. That should remind me to watch where I'm stepping. Lost sight of that pine tree, but I'm still all right.

The going is a little easier now. The land is higher to the right—that's east—better check that.

Well! What do you know about that? North seems to have moved a little farther west of where it's supposed to be. Maybe I'm not holding the compass just right—or am I sighting wrong—some of the charts say there are "local magnetic disturbances" in this area of Upper Michigan. Iron ore deposits cause that "disturbance". There aren't any deposits around here. I don't think there are.

The land seems to be sloping away toward the north-northwest. That would mean that the rocky ridge is probably to the south-southeast. The rocky ridge is supposed to be to the east. What's happening?

Looking back at the higher land just behind and to the right of my course, there's a large rock outcropping.

That rock is the size of a small hotel so it's a sure thing someone didn't just put it there.

I had better bear off more toward north than I have been, especially since north is farther west than I thought it to be. (Is this making sense to you? It was a little cloudy to me just then too.)

I'm moving again. My mind is speculating on how much usable light time remains, just in case I had to select a place to build a fire and gather enough wood to last the night. There wouldn't be any question that a person could survive this night in the bush. A fire would make it more comfortable, but I would prefer the cabin with a warm bunk and the flickering light from the fireplace dancing on the ceiling.

The woods don't seem as friendly as they were—they're more impersonal. Some of the brush seems to have developed a belligerent attitude toward my passing at all. Small twigs, nearly invisible in the fading light, suddenly lash out and sting my cheek. If someone were following me, I'm sure they would notice that my tracks had become noticeably farther apart. I'm not running you understand. This stage is just "heightened concern."

Where the heck am I? The individual trees stand silently and aloof from my problem. They seem to be saying, "Excuse me, but you seem to have mistaken me for someone who gives a damn." The woods are not as friendly as they were.

A decision is necessary! Check the wristwatch. O.K.! If I haven't come upon something recognizable within the next ten minutes, the attempt to find the skidding trail will cease. I'll select a spot and start gathering wood for the night. It won't be so bad. I've got the three fish.

There was a fellow I heard of who got 'hold of a couple of fish and some loaves of bread and fed a whole bunch of folks. I guess, with three fishes, I can feed me.

The decision had been made and the concern (call it panic, if you wish) level diminishes considerably. The biggest hazard to be overcome in any situation of this sort is the tendency toward panic; the only solution seems to be to get out of here—to get away—run! Sometimes it helps to start by assuming the worst that you feel could happen. Anything after that is an improvement.

There's nothing in these north woods of Michigan that's going to "eat you." Face it! A person is in a greater risk situation on a modern highway than asleep in a pile of leaves in the woods. It might get chilly. There'll be noises that are difficult to explain—especially if an active imagination is operating. Look at it from an animal's point of view; they're not looking for a problem. Just living out there in that "jungle" is problem enough.

All the wildlife I have met, and I've been fortunate to have traveled some, are very pragmatic. If they can't eat it, and it's not mating season, they tend to avoid whatever might cause them any sort of inconvenience. During the mating season, the males are competing with each other. Even then the differences are more ceremonial than they are pain inflicting. The winner is determined through a system of mutual consent, and the loser retires to grow some or live out the remainder of his life.

Face it! The animal world doesn't have any great regard for "Homo sapiens" (that's us) one way or the other. They really don't care. Think about that; they're not vindictive! There's no desire for "revenge." There's less to fear from animals than there is from our fellow man. Folks are afraid of things they don't understand; the "unknown." The fact that there's nothing out there that wants to hurt us or have anything to do with us is one of the "unknowns."

About six minutes after my "ten minutes or camp out" decision, I practically fall onto the skidding trail I have been looking for. I hadn't seen it from a distance. If it had been say thirty minutes later, I might have crossed it in the gathering 'darkness and never have known that it was there. A little panic, and I could have crossed it just now.

Concern can cloud awareness. How many of us have been going somewhere, deep in thought, and been unaware of our progress? Even to the point of driving past our destination. When panic has control of the mind, a person is out of it.

Strange tales have come out of the woods, some witnessed to by parties not involved. Rescuers have had to chase a "lost" individual who walked right by them. They had to lead him back to the "real world." The lost individual had reached the point where they didn't know which way was "out" but they were in a hurry to get there. Disoriented and panic-stricken people have run right off steep bluffs, injuring themselves severely. I don't know of anyone "lost" who was hurt in any way by animals.

Once I had found the skidding trail, I immediately knew where I had been and I could have come very close to taking the same track I just came out on and returned to the beaver pond. Not tonight, but in daylight. All this reorientation flooded in with only one foot on the skidding trail. The woods no longer seemed passive and disinterested.

That leaning yellow birch beside the trail is the friendly marker that regularly tells me how far it is to the main trail. Suddenly, all is well. Thirty minutes from now I will be putting a little heat to a pot of stew, I'll be sitting in front of the fireplace, and thinking very little about a night I almost spent in the woods.

I have no doubt that the same thing will happen to me again. Anyone who enjoys "...a small cabin...nearest neighbor is about two and a half miles...watching trout rising to early flies..." is traveling where there are no paths; in the company of those individuals who have been "lost" or who are going to be "lost." For those who travel away from the beaten path, that's the way it is.

The only "enemy" out there is panic. Control the panic. You may get hungry; you may get cold; you may even get scared; that's permitted. As long as panic doesn't get ten feet tall, you'll be all right.

Now! Go on out for a hike in the woods "where there is no path" and enjoy it.

♎

"In Nature there are neither rewards nor punishment there are only consequences"

Robert B. Ingersoll

Life is Not a Destination

SUNRISE

It's quiet. The air is clean. There's no wind - still asleep I guess. The big lake is flat, mirror like. A slight swell slips quietly, gently, onto the beach - and back. Lake Superior may sleep but it's always "breathing" - a slight rising and falling - always.

Sunrise is a beautiful time of day. A person can feel alone, a kind of "oneness" with the world and God and whatever. Maybe that's part of what makes it beautiful.

Those who are about at sunrise; truck drivers flexing stiff muscles, a night-shift worker sleepily heading home to bed, a policeman grabbing a quick cup of coffee, it's a brief moment of privacy, of introspection, a pause.

One person may watch as the sun's rim just breaks the horizon. Another admires the brightening, changing blue of the sky; another watches the contrast between the blue of the sky and the darker blue of the water. Someone else sees the first rays of sunlight touching the top of a tree or a building. It may be for several minutes or it may be as brief as a moment. That thought, that momentary impression, would stay a precious gem, in the jewelbox of memory.

Not all mornings are like this. Sometimes the breaking light of day struggles over the horizon, fighting to penetrate thick clouds and bad weather. On days like that the light just seems to arrive. Those overcast days make the clear mornings even more precious.

As I watch stars fade, they just seem to disappear. A few stray clouds change from gold to red, then to pink and to white. It's going to be a good day.

The sun's rays, reaching over the horizon, first lighten the sky high up. The calm water reflects the changing shades of blue. Then, as the earth rotates, the golden beams dip lower brushing tree tops, mountains, gradually descending down to the cattails in the marsh, and finally to the beach and the street.

We get to enjoy it more because sunrise takes longer in our northern latitudes. The reason involves an angular thing. It has to do with the earth's rotation and the sun's north-south position. By the equator a few degrees of rotation result in the same (nearly) few degrees of sun angle. Further north that same few degrees of rotation bring a lesser change in elevation. We get the sunrise in slow(er) motion.

Sunsets are that way too - slower. The activities of the day, the heating of the earth and the expansion of the atmosphere set the air currents to moving about. Wind blows. Air currents rise. The dust and other pollutants suspended in the atmosphere can create spectacular sunsets. We, in Marquette, are fortunate to have sunset point at Presque Isle. There are other places but sunset point is easily accessible and a comfortable spot from which to watch.

Whoever said "night falls" hadn't seen it happen from an airplane. If you ask a pilot, a flyer, they'll tell you that night doesn't "fall," it oozes up out of the ground. The first places to get dark are the valleys, the deep woods and the low spots. As the sun slides below the horizon darkness creeps into the shadows, up the shaded side of a mountain, slips in between tall trees - buildings. From the air a person can see this happen. As the last peak surrenders the final glint of sunlight, the earth, now covered by its own shadow, surrenders to the darkness. The cockpit of my airplane is still bright with sunshine. On the earth below man-made lights have been winking on. Those automatic vapor lamps, yard lights, come on by themselves popping up at unexpected places far from cities and villages. Pools of light mark the location of night football or a late baseball game. In the winter months, when darkness comes before factory quitting times, rivers of flowing headlights mark expressways as people drive home. If it were needed, that is visual proof of the power and wealth of the oil industry.

Flying over the Mississippi and Ohio rivers at night the tugs and barges are "pointed out" by the powerful beams of their spotlights. They use these fingers of light to see each other and to identify the rivers navigational buoys and markers.

As the sun sinks still further I, too, have to turn on the lights for the flight instruments so I don't lose my way. External navigation lights are turned on so, like the barges on the river, a fellow sojourner and I don't collide. No, night doesn't fall; it chases the retreating sun rising up from the ground to displace the light. The sun's light rises too, into "the heavens" or wherever. In the morning the darkness will flee over the horizon or settle into the valleys, the shadows, the low spots. It'll soak right into the ground. So, you see, it's not the darkness that falls it's the light.

It's amazing how it all works. Science explains, theorizes, says "it must have happened thus and so" with molecules and algae and evolving bits of protoplasm. From the simple act of just being able to wiggle my finger to those select mornings when I sit and watch the sun rise, molecules and protoplasm just don't seem adequate to explain it all.

Ω

THE STALKING OF THE TROUT

"The last Saturday in April."

That's all there is to it. Just open a conversation with that statement. You will immediately gain an insight to whomever you're talking with. If your companion responds with a blank expression you'll know he's one of the unfortunates. Change the subject. Don't make fun of him or embarrass him further. They're more to be pitied than ridiculed. They are not among the chosen, the selected few, those of us who have more than a passing acquaintance with the stalking of the trout.

Aah, the brook trout - "Brookie," to devotees. We recognize "The last Saturday in April" as opening day of trout season in the state of Michigan. And what a fine day it is.

The weather? What's the weather got to do with it? It's the first day of trout season. Unless there's a life threatening blizzard or the country is under nuclear attack the faithful will be out there. They'll be on the bank of a stream somewhere - maybe in pairs, maybe three, or maybe they'll be alone. They'll all be performing those age-old sacred rites and rituals. These chosen few are members of a religious sect as old as man, the followers of the trout.

To know the trout is to love it. It lives in clear, cold, pure water. It won't abide anywhere else. It doesn't subscribe to industries public relations press releases or the state or the federal government's "within legal limits" edicts, or to anybody else. It has no interest in the scientific analysis of "parts per million" of pollutant or "harmless" waste discharge. If the water's not pure the trout is not there. It's up to people like us, you and I, we favored few, who promise to ". . . love, honor, and protect . . ." it in exchange for the pure pleasure it provides us. Remain on guard against the contemporary forces of expediency. When man chooses to "adjust" the environment for material gain, when the condition has progressed to the point where someone says, "I'm sorry," it's too late. The time for protection has already passed. As with the protection of freedom, eternal vigilance is the price we must pay.

Ah but today is opening day! Anticipation is high. There's still snow in sheltered spots in the woods in the Upper Peninsula. It's a little cool. You try to find a sheltered spot where that chilly breeze can't get you. Pick a spot on the river (or creek) bank where the sun hits full. Sit right down - on the ground, if necessary. When you're fishing everything should move at a slow and easy pace. Soak up a little of that sunshine as you join the rod sections, thread the line through the rod-eyes and check the action of the reel. You might pause to stare at the water, reminisce about opening days gone by, dream of that really big one that's lying in wait. This is your life you're living – right here and now! That's something we're inclined to overlook in the hustle and bustle of the day. A person's got to remember that life is not a destination - it's the journey. Take the time to enjoy.

Attach a low breaking-strength leader. Too many fishermen (and women) worry about losing equipment to snags. Get the proper mindset before you wet a line. Say to yourself, "I'm going to lose a hook or two, or a fly, to whatever gods there be that adjudicate the courting of the trout." Once you accept this fact as gospel - and it is Gospel - you'll be amazed at how much more enjoyable fishing becomes.

Now tie on a hook. Whether you use flies or worms,

use a small hook; a number 10 is just fine. This is not Moby Dick the Great White Whale you're after. The trout more easily swallows a tiny hook. The percentage of catches per nibble or per strike will go up. It's your decision whether to use a barbed hook or a smooth one. We'll talk more about that later.

There are many arguments concerning fly-fishing. One of the questions is, "What did the trout know - and when did he know it?" There is a school that says the fly will attract the fish, cause it to strike. Then, through a sensing mechanism - smell or taste - the trout will know that this is not a valid bug and will spit it out. That school says you must keep the fly in sight - or have a sensitive feel for a wet fly - and set the hook quickly. The other argument says the fish doesn't smell or taste and will swallow whatever attracts it. With a worm, the point is moot. Either way, the argument for a small hook, in my opinion, is a valid one.

Before offering your enticement scout the water. Select a likely looking spot, somewhere where the current seems to be wafting whatever goodies are flowing downstream past a sheltered backwater. A trout will pick such a spot, a spot where it can lie quiet without expending much effort while it awaits its lunch. The passing supermarket display allows it to pick and choose whatever appeals to it. There should be a little shade over the spot too. An overhanging branch or, maybe, a sunken log it can get under, or both.

The object is to surreptitiously drift your offering in

a very natural manner to that trout that's lurking in that secluded spot. You're trying to make it an offer it can't refuse. This is real artistry we're discussing here and it takes skill and practice.

My grandfather, many years ago, was instructing me on the finer points of trout fishing. He told me that the trout is a very wary creature. It's easily spooked. Heavy footfalls on the riverbank will be sensed through its lateral line, that line down its sides. A sudden shadow on the water will scare it. A fishing pole waving over the stream will set it off, even a "guv'mint pole" (an alder branch we kids used to cut and tie our lines onto). He advocated crawling those last few feet to the riverbank, quietly, on your belly. I was with him 'til he got to the "crawl on your belly" part. I was thinking that if someone saw me I'd be embarrassed. You've gotta remember I was just a youngster back then. Years later, while taking part in a military survival exercise, we made camp one evening - hot and tired and dusty and hungry enough to tackle the south end of a north bound skunk. There was a little creek nearby. I remembered my grandfather's advice. I tied some nylon thread to the end of an alder branch, bent a pin, and hooked on a grub. I slithered up to that creek on my belly like a snake. I also ate fish that night. Thank you, Grandfather.

Back to our creek.

You'll want to be as crafty as you can about selecting likely fishing holes, judging current flow, and selecting how and where to float your bait. Do you need a little split-shot sinker - or not? Maybe a small float, a bobber? These are judgment calls. No one can tell you what to do. Nobody really knows. Everybody is guessing. The only way to avoid mistakes is through experience. The only way to get experience is by making mistakes. What more can I say?

If you encounter a possible snag the smaller hook once more has an advantage. It is less likely to catch on a twig or branch. If it does snag, that light leader will avoid your re-arranging the whole riverbank getting your line loose. It'll give way and break early on. With a little luck, you won't even scare the fish. So you lose a hook. Big deal! Don't run your blood pressure up over a piece of bent wire and a dead twig.

Once you've got everything going your way, the current is drifting your offering right to the spot. Maybe you can still see your dry fly - maybe not. The leader should now be invisible to eliminate the appearance of the bait tied to something. Neither you nor the fish is supposed to see it. The line, on the other hand, can be a visible thing. I like a line I can see. As the bait moves out of my sight - ten or fifteen feet away - I watch the line drifting along in loops and whorls. When that trout makes its move - streaks out from his secluded hiding place, seizes the bait, and darts back - that drifting line will suddenly shoot out straight, pointing to where the action is.

That's when your eyes pop open wide. Adrenaline surges into the system. I can just feel that fish "chewing" on that bait clear up through the line and the rod and into my arm. Gather up the loose line - quickly but don't jerk it. Gently, steadily, raise the tip of the rod, overhanging branches permitting, and give a slight quick tug. You'll either feel the jerks and twitches of a hooked fish - or your offering will retrieve sadly and easily. There's another option: that clever little dude may have wrapped your line around a snag. If you're snagged, back up a couple paragraphs and read it again. Get your lure back - or re-bait your hook - and try it again. Now you know the fish was in there. Maybe it's still hungry? If you have no immediate luck, move on - but remember the spot for later.

If you've hooked the fish, it'll try to reach a hole or brush or cover somewhere. Remember, you've got that light leader so don't try to "horse" the thing around. Don't "horse" it anyway - be gentle. You want to "feel" what is happening and you can't do that when your muscles are tense. Guide that fish away from those spots as best you can. This is the real enjoyment, the matching of wits and the pleasure of fishing. There's a contest here that makes the whole expedition, the cold weather, the wet feet, the hook-in-the-finger, it makes it all worthwhile.

Finally you've got a tired trout in the shallows, probably lying on its side, exhausted. You can scoop it up, admire it, the coloration, the spots, the clean smooth lines. That fish is a thing of beauty. Maybe you take a picture of it lying in the green grass on the riverbank.

Now, are you going to put it in the creel and take it home? Later you can clean it, fry it in butter - it makes me drool just thinking about that. Fry it in real butter and to heck with the cholesterol.

Maybe you decide to "catch and release" as they say. If you intend to release it, plan your moves to minimize the fish's time out of the water. If the hook is in the lip, especially if it's a smooth, not a barbed hook, it will be more easily undone. This is where some prefer to file off the barb, use a smooth hook. I simply take a pair of needle nose pliers and pinch the barb flat against the body of the hook. Without a barb sticking out the hook can be removed more easily. The down side of this is that the fish may throw the smooth hook before you land it, too. Suit yourself. Wet your hands before picking the fish up - and don't squeeze very hard. It makes it harder for you but a lot easier on the fish. Maybe it swallowed that little number ten hook right down its gullet - maybe just part way. If there's a question that removing it might injure the fish, just cut the line, close up to the fishes mouth. Leave the hook where it is - even if it's sticking out of its mouth a bit. The digestive juices in the fish will dissolve the hook. It'll be all right. The number ten hook is not only small, it's shank and all is small - easier to dissolve than a heavier hook.

Don't "throw" the fish back in. Gently place the fish in the shallows. If it's slow in taking off, move it forward and backward just a little. The fish being out of water is like you or I being under water. It may need a little

"CPR" to recover. Once it comes 'round, a little puff of sand in the water will be all that remains. The fish will have flipped its tail and taken off. You may stare at the spot, watch the sand settle and remember the "catch." Most of us do. That clear cold water flows by. You're left with a cold wet hand and a warm memory.

Go find that sheltered spot on the riverbank in the sunshine. Lay back on the grass with the warm sun shining down and the river, that cold clear water flowing by. If you brought a thermos of coffee - or a cold beer - now is the time. Relax! Enjoy! Life is the journey - and this is it.

Life is Not a Destination

Summer

MEMORIES ARE MADE OF THIS

I was up to Big Bay for the Ice Fishing Derby a while ago. Among the fish caught were several large northern pike. Looking at them, the large mouth, the teeth, the staring eyes, brought back a memory - and that brought other memories.

If you're younger than 50 or 55 the rest of this might not mean much to you. Maybe you could go have a bowl of pablum while your parents and I talk?

I guess it had to be in the 1930s. It was during a period in the country's history now known as the "Great Depression." Many people were out of work. Money was tight. If you think we're recycling now, you should have seen us back then.

My grandparents owned some land on the north side of Lake Autrain down toward Munising in Michigan's Upper Peninsula. My dad and a couple of my uncles had built a cabin on the shore. I was, I guess, six years old - somewhere around there.

Dad was a policeman on the Marquette City Police Force. He got a vacation each summer during the last two weeks in July. The family would plan that vacation trip "to the lake" for weeks beforehand. Mom handled the clothes and the groceries. Dad organized the tools and fishing equipment. I, mostly, just got in the way.

These days folks may run from Marquette down to Munising for a quick lunch. It didn't used to be that way. With the car all packed and "riding on the axles," it took us the better part of the day to get from Marquette to the lake. Maybe we'd go down to Carlshend and cut across through Chatham. Maybe we'd turn at Beaver Grove, go through Mangum, Deerton, and Onota. 'Most all the roads were dirt or gravel and if you didn't encounter a hole that buried you clean out of sight you considered it a pretty good road. There was no M-28 or paving and thirty miles per hour was "high speed." As I remember, the county would often spread – calcium I think? - on the dirt roads to "keep the dust down." Which of the roads we decided to take could depend on whether it had rained recently. It was a day long adventure whichever way we went.

When we got to the camp, I couldn't wait to run down to the shore. Mom and dad would unpack the car and evaluate what maintenance had to be done right away and what could be put off. I'd probably get my feet wet. Nobody cared. We were "at camp." The rules were off. Well, many of the rules were anyway.

Mom would clean the camp. Dad would check the condition of the outhouse. Another must-do right away job was priming the hand water pump. It took a bit of doing. The pump leathers had to "soak," to swell up in the brass cylinder so they'd create a vacuum strong enough to raise water from the well point some eighteen or twenty feet down in the sand.

At camp summer evenings were long and lazy. When it got dark we'd light kerosene lamps for light. The kerosene lamp would cast huge dark shadows on the walls. A friendly fire would crackle in the fireplace and make everything cozy.

The days would pass with me searching the woods for Indians, chasing rabbits in the swamp, swimming, and fishing on the lake with dad. We had a rowboat and an outboard motor. Sometimes mom would come with us and sometimes she'd stay at camp and work jigsaw puzzles - or go for walks. There were only eight or ten cabins on the whole lake back then. The world was ours.

One afternoon we'd been across the lake, fishing in a bay. Deciding to go back to the cabin, we had raised the anchor and just let the boat drift lazily along. Dad let his fishing line trail along behind. Suddenly he got a bite, a real genuine "hit." The brake on dad's fishing reel squealed as the fish stripped line off of it. Abruptly things went from lazy, warm, and sleepy to wide-eyed and alert. Dad grabbed his fishing pole and tried to control the loss of line. The rod bent almost double. Excitement flowed through the boat like electricity.

He worked the fish slowly, giving line, retrieving line and gradually bringing the fish to the boat. I was all eyes, right there, hanging over the side of the boat. Mom had 'hold of my shirt to be sure I didn't fall in. I was watching where that line went into the water, cutting and swishing back and forth as that fish resisted. Then it happened!

The biggest monster I'd ever seen in my life came up out of the depths. It was green with staring eyes and a great gaping jaw. It was looking straight at me. I don't know if I wet my pants or not. Our boat had a small enclosed cowl in the bow. I let out a yelp and headed for the protection of that forward cowl. There was a small entry door. I was through it like a shot.

Equally startled by the sudden appearance of that fish and by my reaction, mom was yelling at dad to cut the line. She tried to coax me out of that hole. Neither dad nor I were doing what she wanted.

Dad had gotten a look at the monster he had hooked and he wasn't about to let it go. I was "hid," safe, and wasn't going to move. Mom - she always was the smartest one in our family - quickly surmised that under the cowling was probably the best place for me at the moment. She saw dad wasn't about to give up the fight and turned to help him. Dad had a gaff-hook aboard the boat and finally hauled Moby Dick aboard. It flopped a bit inside the boat 'til he clipped it a sharp rap between the eyes with a wrench. It took a while before I finally came out of my hole.

Those were my thoughts, my memories as I looked at that big pike at Big Bay. I don't remember the size of dad's fish - it was BIG. As little as I was at the time I probably remember it as even bigger. There were those same huge jaws, those teeth, those same eyes.

I've been down to Lake Autrain since, looking over the old camp from the road, remembering. Someone else owns it now. They've added rooms but the basic camp is still there. I wonder if they know any of the history of the place? There are many stories inside those walls.

The word was that Al Capone and his boys used to come up here from Chicago - to "cool off" it was said. He and/or his "boys" stayed in a resort across the lake, spent most of their time playing cards in their cabin. That was the story anyway.

I remember another fall weekend the family was here. Mom had brought some meat for our Sunday meal and had stored it in a stone crock on the little back porch. That evening she heard noise on the back porch. Opening the door, lantern in hand, she found a bear trying to get into the crock. Remember now, this was during the depression. Groceries were hard to come by, especially meat. That was the family's dinner that bear was trying to steal.

Mom grabbed the broom and was out the door after that bear, swatting and shouting "Git!" Dad, hearing the commotion, jumped up to see what was wrong.

"Geeezus Bertha! That's a bear you're after. Let 'im go!" I've heard many stories of people and bear and bravery and tragedy but this encounter was no contest. That bear headed for the tall timber. My own experiences with animals along the way have led to my own theories on how and what and why they do what they do. I believe animals can tell when a person is afraid and tend to act accordingly. Mom wasn't scared that night and that bear knew it.

Out back was another cabin, a small one-room log place that had been built in later years. My folks used to rent out the main cabin during the summer and had wanted a place to spend a weekend or two themselves.

Dad's job as a policeman used to put him in contact with quite a cross section of humanity. Lumberjacks passing through town often found themselves broke, night coming on, and nowhere to stay. Frequently the police department, if there was no one in the jail at the time, would allow a 'jack, down on his luck, to sleep in a cell - but just for one night.

My father was of Finnish descent and had the idea that anyone who was Scandinavian just naturally knew how to build a log cabin. One old time lumberjack, Gus (some Nordic name), found himself spending a night courtesy of the City of Marquette.

He and Dad got to talking about one thing and another and a deal was struck: Dad would provide a place for Gus to stay including something to eat and Gus would build dad a log cabin. The next morning Gus found himself on the shore of Lake Autrain with groceries, tools, and a load of logs.

After a week or two we all went down to see how the cabin was progressing. They weren't. A few of the logs had been shuffled around and a sort of foundation had been arranged but things were moving pretty slow. Dad pitched in to help and get things moving. Now and then he would turn to Gus with a question. It didn't seem to dawn on Dad that he, too, was Scandinavian and, by his own assumption, was supposed to know how to build a cabin too.

When a question was asked - I can close my eyes today and still see this - Gus would get this contemplative expression, fold his left arm across his stomach, hold his right elbow in his left hand, rub his chin with his right hand, and say, "Vell, now, let me t'ink."

Gus didn't know any more about building cabins than my Dad did. In the end, between the two of them, they got the job done and the cabin they built is standing yet today.

Other camps and cabins have sprung up all around Lake Autrain since then. Some of what today's owners call "camps" are pretty palatial mansions. There's commercial electric power, paved roads, telephones, air conditioning and on and on.

Seaplanes take off and land on the lake during the summer. It's not the Lake Autrain I knew. I've got my memories though – nobody can change them.

The only thing constant is change. I guess it's true: a person can never "go back home."

♎

"Life is what's happening while you are making other plans."

Unknown

AFTER THE STORM

The little cabin up by the Yellow Dog River is my own private get-a-way. It's a good place to go when there's some heavy thinking to be done. It's a good place to go to get away from heavy thinking. It's just a good place to go. It provides a sort of "mind decongestant."

Up in the bush I'm able to get away from everybody and everything. I don't have to look out my window into my neighbor's kitchen. Wait a minute! You'd better hold that comment. I guess I do look into my "neighbor's" kitchen, come to think of it. My "neighbors" are a family of beaver. There are other wildlife neighbors too but they don't all live as close as the beaver.

I wanted to build a small dam on the little creek that passes the camp. I found out there are all kinds of laws and rules about that. The beaver god must have heard my mutterings and sent those beaver to grant my wish. I added a desk and a chair - an "office" - down beside the pond. Maybe that was too much. The beaver built the dam higher. And the water, well, you know. I would have been wet up to my - er - dignity.

I do like to sit on a bench by the pond. It's peaceful there. I watch the cedar waxwings flit back and forth catching flies and bugs in flight. In spring and early summer a family of ducks may show themselves - if I'm very quiet for a time. I've got to be quiet to see the beaver, too. They don't usually come out 'til evening, right at last light. It's usually the little ripples on the smooth water in the evening – "when the wind has grown tired and is still"- that betray their presence. Those ripples are the give away. You know, a person just can't watch those unassuming animals and worry at the same time.

Sitting by the pond watching and listening I try to identify the individual sounds and the sights and read what I can into them. There's duckweed in the pond. I wonder where it came from? I didn't plant it. Do you think, maybe, the ducks did? Maybe they carried it in stuck to their feet? or their feathers? It had to come from somewhere?

I don't think it's important whether I know the names

of the plants and animals to enjoy them. It's nice if you do to be able to talk to someone else about them. That way a person can enjoy the experience again. Maybe I'll try to remember to look them up - or guess at them.

While I sat wondering and speculating I hadn't noticed how quiet it's gotten. The cedar waxwings have disappeared. There's no wind. Everything is quiet and still - like it's waiting for something. The sun has hidden its face behind an approaching cloud. I look up and see that it's a big dark cumulous cloud. It's getting closer. It's getting darker. In the distance I hear a faint sound like frying bacon. Nothing is moving. Even the raucous cry of the blue jay is still. The leaves of the quaking aspen that quiver in the slightest breeze are motionless. So am I. I know what's coming. I know - but I don't move. The anticipation, the watching, the listening is enjoyment.

It's rain! Rain is coming! It's been dry and hot. A nice cooling rain will be welcome. The sizzling is getting louder. Suddenly a cool breath of wind washes over me. Small patches of ripples – I've heard them called "cat's paws" – brush across the pond. The aspen leaves quiver and twist slightly. The woods seem to heave a collective sigh. Then a maple leaf flinches in surprise as a drop of water hits it. The surface of the pond shows a dot here, then another there, then six or twelve more. The dots expand and overlap. Soon the pond is spackled with them.

The air has cooled considerably. The temperature

has definitely dropped. The rain drops are not just more numerous now but they're larger. The sizzle grows into a roar. The cabin is 300, maybe 400 feet away. It's time to take cover.

The front porch is screened and I swing the door open on the run and duck under the eave. Water running off the roof is chortling into an empty water bucket. The raindrops hitting the tin roof rattle a musical tattoo. I flop down into an old overstuffed chair on the porch - a chair that must be as old as I am - and just enjoy watching and listening to the rain.

It's darker now. I didn't see a lightning flash but I hear the thunder. My grandmother used to tell me that thunder was the sound of the "brownies playing ten pins." It satisfied the fears of a scared little boy. I think of her whenever I hear it.

When rain comes like this, sudden, intense, large drops, it means it's probably from a cumulous cloud passing over and it won't last long. As I speculate that it will probably be a short rain I notice it's already letting up. It's already growing noticeably brighter. The drenched forest sort of sags under the weight of the water clinging to leaves, branches, ferns. The rat-tat-tat on the tin roof slackens. The rush of water into the rain bucket slows but continues. The air is fresh and cool.

Gradually the sun peeks out from behind the clouds. The colors in the woods, the greens and grays and blacks and browns, the flowers, all seem brighter, clearer, sharper. The sunshine turns the droplets of water on the leaves and the pine needles into sparkling diamonds. I sit quietly, breathing deep of the clean air. Everything is fresh and new again.

♎

Life is Not a Destination

THE BEACH RETREAT

"Gee, wouldn't it be nice if . . ."

That's how it all started. Relaxing with a cup of coffee while looking across the bayou at Lake Superior in one of its more argumentative moods. "Wouldn't it be nice if we could sit on the beach and watch those waves roll in?"

"Not me! It's too cold out there."

"Well, it's no time to be out there in a canoe."

"It'd be even worse to be out there without one."

Silence while Dorothy and I meditated on these profound observations. "Suppose," said I, "that you could sit out there in a shelter? like a greenhouse?"

"Ummh."

I knew the conversation was over - but the thought persisted. Not about the canoe, but about the greenhouse thing. There'd be the lumber to buy - and the windows, geez, windows are expensive. And maybe the lake would just roll up and wash the thing away - or blow it down. And then there's the zoning - a building permit. I seem to recall that, in Chocolay Township, they won't let a person build closer than fifty feet or so from the high water mark. There were all kinds of reasons why not - but the thought persisted.

We had built a floating bridge and a marsh walk to the beach. We had to cross 800 or 900 feet of bayou and marsh. I'm kind of proud of that walk. It started out with a pencil, a piece of paper and a little pocket calculator. It's all been done in accord with Department of Natural Resources and Department of Environmental Quality recommendations. How long are the spans? What can I float the bridge on? How much is it going to cost? How much weight can an empty fifty-gallon drum in the water support? How many drums will I need? How much will they cost? Where can I get the drums? How much will they cost? And most important overall, how much is it going to cost?

It took most of one summer but now it's there. I even had an artist stop by one day and ask if I would allow her to paint a picture of my bridge. How about that?

We've used the beach more in six weeks after it was

completed than we had in the preceding six years. A beach house would be nice addition. A "Beach Retreat." A place to escape the telephones and the television and the . . . I wonder if I couldn't find some way to . . .?

I was talking to Richard Wilder one day, at "Wilder's Glass and Collectibles" in Marquette. He asked if I knew anyone who wanted a really good deal on some thermo pane windows. It seems that he had a job involving the removal and replacement of windows and had the "used" windows on his hands.

Do you believe in signs? Coincidence? You know, like "extrasensory perception" and things like that? I may "knock wood" or toss salt over my shoulder but the way this was happening was almost spooky.

Another obstacle could be the Chocolay Township zoning ordinance. I called on Mark Maki at the township office. Mark advised me that a building that close to the water wouldn't be permitted - BUT! - if the building was under 100 square feet it wouldn't come under that law. How about that? Lessee, if I made it 8' x 12', that would be - times two - carry the one - and that comes out . . . Well, it'd be less than 100 square feet.

I had an old telephone pole I'd scrounged from somewhere. Being a child of hard times, raised during the great depression, I find it hard to throw anything away – or to turn down anything I could wildly imagine having a use for. I could probably cut that treated telephone pole into four-foot lengths and bury them vertically deep in the sand as foundation posts. With the windows from

Wilders, the walls could be almost all glass. I began to see my castle rising.

There was (and still is) a lot more I don't know about building than I do. Ah, but what wonders have been accomplished by people who don't know what they can't do. ". . .and he started right in with the trace of a grin on his face – if he worried, he hid it. And he started to sing as he tackled the thing that couldn't be done – and he did it!" There's a deity that protects fools and the innocent and it has been by my side quite often.

Folks who sell lumber just "sell lumber." They don't ask if you know what you're doing. I threw around a few words like "footings" and "floor joists" and "rafters," words I had heard the big guys say. It seemed to work - but I suspect they knew.

The roof was going to be tin - steel, actually. There's no musical symphony in the world as beautiful as the sound of rain on a tin roof in the darkness at night.

Neighbors stopped by, as neighbors are wont to do. Some asked about building permits. Some speculated on the wrath of the "Big Lake" rising up to swallow my creation. Some seemed to like the idea - and some not.

It was too late! By now I was taken with the same zeal that must have possessed Doctor Frankenstein. "Come, Igor, we have work to do!" I was creating! I was making something that had never been! Igor never showed up but I managed to "create" without him.

Now that's there too, my creation, the "Beach

Retreat," and it's beautiful! I'm sitting there now, out on the beach as I write this. A pale sun shines low in the western sky. A gentle south wind carries with it a touch of fall. It's so quiet and peaceful out here a person never wants to leave – ever. Unless you've been there it's hard to believe.

So what'll I do if the lake rises up and smites the place? What could I do? Maybe I'm a little fatalistical and superstitious but look at all the disassociated events that fell into place to make this happen. It's almost as if it were meant to be.

And what if it wasn't meant to be? Well, we'll cross that bridge when we come to it.

Ω

*"If you think you can
or if you think you can't,
you're probably right."*

Henry Ford

Life is Not a Destination

EVERYTHING OLD IS NEW AGAIN

The guy was, I don't know, in his late twenties I would guess. I was to discover that he was divorced. He had "visitation" - I guess that's what they call it - with his son, a lad eight years old or so. I don't remember their names. They had come to Big Bay in Upper Michigan for an outdoor adventure. They were going to "camp out" at Perkins Park.

It was a beautiful day. Spring was here. Fresh new buds were bursting out everywhere. Wildflowers were popping up in riotous profusion. It was one of those spring days when the warm sun just wraps itself right around you. Fishermen and hikers and campers, sensing liberation from the long drawn out bonds of an icy winter, were scrambling all over each other in their rush to enjoy the weekend. Everyone wanted to taste the miracle of resurrection that occurs every spring in the North Country.

Perkins Park was full. The fella with the little boy didn't have a reservation. He and his son retreated to the Big Bay Café where daddy was trying to come up with something – anything. That's where I got involved. I couldn't help but overhear the daddy struggling to explain the situation to his young son.

That daddy had my sympathy even though I didn't

fully understand how or why he did what he had done. He's got no reservations. He hadn't planned the weekend very well. But he is a daddy struggling to create a few precious memories with his son in the few days he has. This guy's planning might indicate he was a brick or two short of a full load but that's probably why I identified with him. Never mind the hows and the whys of that seemingly fraternal relationship. Psychiatrists get wealthy explaining guys like us to ourselves.

During a lapse in their conversation I caught the daddy's eye. I grinned, nodded, and opened a conversation. "Beautiful day, isn't it?"

He responded with a nod and a brief effort at a slight smile. The youngster turned his head to see who was doing the talking. He cautiously looked me over.

"D'ya like ice cream?" I ask.

He looks questioningly at his dad. Who is this guy who wants to know if I like ice cream? Is he some kinda' nut? Everybody likes ice cream. His dad kind of shrugs and nods encouragement. The boy looks back at me.

"D'ya like ice cream?" The answer is a bit of an uncertain nod. I gather he likes ice cream but he's not sure whether he likes me. "Well," I explain, "I happen to know they've got a big tub," I hold my hands out descriptively, "of ice cream back behind the counter. About this time of year, after a long winter, it starts to turn green and they have to throw it away."

His eye's are locked on me, never wavering. "I tell you what. I know the fella' who owns this place and I believe, if we ask him, he'll give you a dish of that ice cream."

The problem has been presented. Ice cream is good. Green is bad. I'm a stranger. What's he to do? He turns to his dad.

Pay attention now. This is a lot like fishing, you know. You have to present the bait in an enticing way and watch the response of the "fish" closely. Maxine White, wife and co-owner is behind the counter listening and watching this happen. She and I and her husband, Dick, are good friends

"Maxine!" I call to her. "Do you still have that green ice cream back there?" The lad and I are both watching for her response. Maxine picks it up with out missing a beat.

"Why, yes. I think we've got a little left." Maxine has been through this casting-maneuvering-enticing presentation with me before. I bring the "lure" closer now, trying to encourage a "hit."

"If you just don't eat the green I think everything will be OK."

You talk about a youngster with a problem, here he is. "Ice cream" is wiggling tantalizingly on the hook but "green" has cast the shadow of doubt. "Why don't you just take a look at it. See what you think." The eyes are back on me again while Maxine struggles to mask her smile. "If you don't want it," I raise my hands to indicate no loss, "why, it hasn't cost a thing." That's a slight twitch of the rod tip. It creates a quiver in that "dry fly" floating enticingly close. One more cautious check with his dad who shrugs noncommittally. He's nibbling! There's a slight nod of his head. A strike! I've got him!

Maxine serves up the ice cream - I believe they call the flavor "Rainbow" - and places the dish before him. "Just be careful," I suggest, "not to eat the green."

His daddy's got a big grin on his face. You can see the light break across the lad's face. He's got it figured out now too. He digs in while Maxine notes the ice cream on my tab.

For you fishermen who haven't been initiated, this is called "catch and release." Try it some time. It doesn't always work but when it does, you can't get better "sport" anywhere.

While my latest "trophy" eats ice cream - green and all - I mention a camping spot I know of to his father. They have a self-contained camper-cap on a small pick up truck. I know a place that's not really open to the public but no one will bother them there. We settle our bill with Maxine and they follow me as I head back to my cabin in the woods.

The spot I had in mind is in a beautiful stand of white birch beside the quiet waters of Bear Lake. The old "two-rut" logging road passes through the birches with a convenient turn-around area that will comfortably accommodate their camper. They'll be right near the shore where they can swim and fish and "adventure" around a campfire. At night an owl may hoot away off in the forest. They'll hear an otter make a mysterious sounding splash in the darkness. A "bear" (a raccoon actually) will crash through the brush. The moon will silently smile down on them. Maybe, in the first light of morning, a doe and a fawn will pause on the shoreline for a drink. Dad will get up and get a warm fire going. A hot cup of chocolate is a perfect way to greet a chilly morning. The whole world looks better from beside a friendly campfire. After leading them to this spot I tell them to enjoy themselves but, when they leave, to be sure they leave nothing behind but tracks.

It was a few days later that the pair of them came by our cabin. They presented Dorothy and I with a fine fish dinner - skinned, filleted, and ready for the pan. The offering was not requested or necessary and, therefore, doubly appreciated.

All this happened several years ago. I pass that camping spot by Bear Lake every time I go up to my cabin on the Yellow Dog River. Every time I pass I remember that daddy and his young son. It's private thought though - a personal thing. Each time I remember I get a warm feeling deep down inside. If I can "catch" a couple more like that why maybe even an old heathen like me might get his foot in St. Peter's door. Best I can figure, after all the bowing and posturing and hymn singing, this is how we're supposed to treat each other.

I take a few minutes to check my creel now and

then, to see what trophies I've caught with my "green ice cream." It's a secret you know. You won't find it in any catalogues or bait shops anywhere. You've got to know how to present it. The whole secret is in the presentation and in having the courage to expose your ego to a possible rebuff. There are times when your best presentations are snubbed, ignored. That's the way it is with anything that's worthwhile in life. The opportunities are there - right in front of you. The only thing worse than being vulnerable – is not being vulnerable. Think about that. The secret's in the presentation.

Autumn

Life is Not a Destination

AND IT WAS GONE . .

I awoke the other morning early. I'm usually in bed by nine PM and am often up before the sun. This particular morning I stumbled half awake into the bathroom and glanced out the window. It was beautiful! The sky was dark and overcast and the bayou in front of the house was in deep shadow. The sun had just broken above the horizon and a solitary ray of clear sunlight shown on a birch tree on the beach. Its leaves had turned to fall's golden color highlighting that single ray of sunshine. I think I experienced what Moses must have felt when that bush caught fire on him - remember that story? Nobody spoke to me out of that tree but the feeling and the thought were there. I just stared at it for maybe a minute or two.

My next thought was to try to get a picture of that. I hurriedly splashed some water on my face, pulled on a sweat suit and a pair of slippers and grabbed my camera on the way to the kitchen door. When I got there – it was gone. The whole world was in shadow. I wondered for a minute if I had actually seen what I had seen but of course I had. It had been there - for a few brief moments – and now it was gone.

Maybe because I'm older – that's the politically correct way of putting it – that I notice such things. It seems a human failing to define "old" as someone at least ten years older than you. I do admit to being nearer to the end of my life than the beginning and that realization inclines a person toward reminiscing, remembering the good times, the adventures, the high points. They all seem to have happened so quickly. I guess everybody wonders at times what would have happened if they had turned left, say, instead of right somewhere along the way. "Two roads diverged in the wood, and I, I took the one . . ." well, the one I took. A person can look back and say it was a mistake, that it was wrong to have gone that way. That's a step into negative thinking and sorrow and depression. Don't do that.

Life's pathway is strewn with decisions and choices. Decide! Choose! Then go that way without regret. Watch for that sunshine. You'll find it in the smile of children, the glow on the face of someone who has encountered good fortune. You'll feel especially good if you had something to do with that child's smile or that adult's good fortune. And don't say anything about it. Keep it to yourself. People who advertise how good they are usually aren't. People who quietly go about living their beliefs, they too become known. And when you know – and you need a friend - you know whom you'll turn to – and why.

The thing about that ray of sunlight is that it was there. All I had to do was look and see it. Had I turned inward – to the mirror for example and stared at my haggard and unshaven face I would have missed it completely. As it is I'll remember that brilliantly lighted golden tree a lot longer than my bleary face in the mirror. But I had to look outward to see it. Maybe there's a message there?

I've got two little grandsons about one year old and four years old. Yes and they own me and they know it and they get whatever they want when they visit. But I try to show them these truths, to start them looking in the right direction. In exchange I bask in the glow of their happiness. Already I notice the changes taking place in my older grandson as he reaches out, testing the world he lives in. I guess the biggest problem grandparents have with grandchildren is that they grow up. They insist on making their own mistakes just like you and I. I hope I've been able to help him along the way.

In life don't focus on the bleary and aged face in the mirror. There are too many specters of what you may or may not have done in the past to live there. If you can't change it, let it go. Don't try to explain or justify.

"This above all: to thine ownself be true and it shall follow, as night follows day, you cannot then be false to anyone."

Shakespeare: Hamlet

That ray of sunshine will brighten your life too.

Ω

Life is Not a Destination

THE WINDS OF MEMORY

The thermometer read 47 degrees this morning. The winds were out of the north at "ten to twenty" according to the weather forecaster. Waves on the lake were hurrying shoreward, grinning as they crashed onto the beach. The waves further out seemed to be smiling in anticipation of their rush onto the sand. Ducks were beginning to flock together. They had gathered in the bayou just below the porch in anticipation of my feeding them.

I dug out a quart or so of whole corn and tossed it into the bayou. Well, most of it made it to the bayou.

With that wind some of it landed in Dorothy's flower garden. Dorothy gets a little upset when the ducks and geese invade her flowers after the corn and do – well, what geese and ducks all too often do. I try to tell her that's what makes the flowers grow but I don't think she's buying that. Oh well it's late in the year and maybe she won't notice. If she does, I'll play innocent as if I didn't know anything about it.

You know, those ducks and geese come right up to the dock when grandson Levi and I go down there to feed them. The geese sort of take over when they're on the scene, neck crooked and head down near water level they'll chase the ducks away. Hunters have to put out decoys, wear camouflage clothing, paint their faces and play tunes on their duck or goose calls to try to attract them and even then the ducks and geese don't always come. How do they know they can swim right up to Levi and me without fear – we could almost pat them on the head – but will steer clear of those hunters? I think they must have something in their heads beside eyeballs.

Back to the original story. Feeding those ducks this morning – the geese were evidently off somewhere else– that north wind went clear through my cotton sweat suit. I didn't stand outside watching for very long. Back inside I closed the door and hurried to the fireplace to stand in front of the open fire. Feeling the radiant heat from that fire brought back memories of our old farmhouse in Harvey and frosty winter mornings. Mom would have been up and started a fire in the kitchen stove. When I got up my bare feet would hit the icy floor, I'd scramble into my shorts, grab my clothes and head for the kitchen. Aah but the heat from the old wood stove felt good. The coffee would be perkin' and, well, life just didn't get much better than that.

There's something special about wood heat. It's warmer, more comfortable than gas-fired central heating systems or electric radiant heat or oil or any of the others. I know that the scientific types will tell you that heat is heat measured in "British Thermal Units" and represent "X" amount of energy that can be converted, transferred or transformed. Darn few of those high-powered intellectuals have scurried across an icy floor to stand beside a toasty warm wood stove on a frosty morning though. Don't misunderstand me. A person should listen when those educated folks talk – they're smart fellas. Just don't send them out to split wood or they're apt to cut their foot off.

The wind and the temperature and the warm fire this morning was a reminder that we live in a land of seasons. The gold and crimson of fall are just a few days away. Then come a few beautiful lazy days of Indian summer. After that the winds will get serious, the mercury in the thermometer will try to hide and that wood fire will really feel good. Even if you don't stand close where the radiant heat can reach you, just gazing into an open fire will warm your heart, especially when it brings back pleasant memories. And then you know that spring is always there.

It was my mother who built this house I now own and live in and where I'm able to feed ducks and geese from the back porch. Not a day goes by that I don't think of her and thank her for her foresight. It's so pleasant, so peaceful looking out across the still waters of the sheltered bayou that I can't help but think it's my mother who "leadeth me beside the still waters and restoreth my soul." Why is it we grow so soon old and so late smart? It's at times like these so late in my life that I realize too that the warmth in that old farmhouse kitchen didn't all come from the wood stove.

THOUGHTS BY A WOODPILE

I've been working in the wood yard, splitting a little kindling and stacking a little firewood against the coming winter. The only use Dorothy and I have for firewood these days is our fireplace. I know a fireplace is inefficient and sucks more heat out of the house than it adds but I like to look at it, to watch the fire. It wasn't always that way. I remember a day not all that long ago when firewood was considered one of the staffs of life. Folks who hadn't laid in an ample supply of firewood before winter would either be cutting wood in the snow or feeling pretty chilly before spring.

Back home on the farm it was my job to keep the wood box beside ma's kitchen stove filled. One night dad came in from the barn and noticed that the wood box wasn't full. I was lying on the floor reading a "Captain Marvel" comic book, something like that.

"The wood box isn't full," he said.

I looked up, irritated at the interruption. "Yeah," I replied. He had broken my imaginary adventure with Captain Marvel. "I'll get it in a minute."

"You'll get it NOW!"

You know, there are times when you can tell from the tone of voice that – well, I knew I had better move – NOW!

You have to visualize this. The coat rack was beside the arch between the kitchen and the living room. Dad was taking his coat off. I was putting my coat on. I glanced up at him with a look something less than the love and adoration a son should feel for his father. He was looking back.

The kitchen was about 14 feet wide with the refrigerator against the far wall. Mom had just opened the refrigerator door. The back of my father's hand sent me across the kitchen and right in amongst the tossed salad we were now going to have for supper. Mom looked up in surprise. I got on out of there and filled the wood box. Nobody said anything but communication had taken place.

My mother filled that wood box for me several times over the years, protecting me from unexpected trips across the kitchen – a fact of which I am not very proud. It was firewood that finally killed my father. He had heart problems. I believe they were from the tensions associated with his job. He had retired as Assistant Chief of the Marquette Police Department. He enjoyed police work and the camaraderie of his fellow officers but there was friction between himself and the guy he worked for. It was a seniority system that placed them working with one another and the other guy was the boss. Anyway dad was now retired and the doctor was telling him he should "slow down." Slow down to the doctor and slow down to my father weren't the same thing. Dad was out by the woodpile chopping wood one afternoon. That was something a person just did when winter was coming on. Feeling tired, he came into the house and sat down in his easy chair. He never got up. I think of my dad whenever I cut firewood.

Now days if a father sent his son across the kitchen and into the refrigerator that way there'd be a lawsuit and charges of child abuse or cruelty. Maybe it wasn't cruelty though. I never doubted that my father loved me. Forgive me, some of you out there, but I really think it's more "abusive" to allow kids to avoid and evade responsibilities rather than impressing upon them – and I use the word "impress" intentionally – the responsibilities that accrue with adulthood.

We seem to have made a lot of progress since "the old

days." Life is easier. Homes are automated and centrally heated. There's no longer a need to cut firewood and fill wood boxes. And the kids now days are growing up – are growing – to be - - you know, I wonder if all the changes are really progress?

Ω

THE FIREPLACE

When the winds of November come howling around the corner the place to be is inside, somewhere warm. The wind lashes the branches and sets them thrashing against one other. Sleet rattles against the windowpane and I shiver just sitting here thinking about it.

I think of folks who have to work out in weather like this, utility repairmen and policemen. My cup of hot chocolate goes down well warming me up inside. The lighthouse on the point at Marquette's lower harbor flashes its clock-regular assigned code. Between that light and I are about five miles of Lake Superior's cold, hostile, angry water. When the big storms roll in they bring waves that can wash clear over the strip of beach between the lake and the bayou. It's a good evening to stay inside, close to the warm, next to the fireplace.

I enjoy a fireplace. I know it's inefficient and sometimes it smokes up the house and my wife may say something about that. And of course you've got to cut wood - or buy it - and there are grates to clean and ashes to haul. When the glass fire doors are open it sucks warm air out of the house. All true but this is a personal thing. I like an open fire, to watch the flames flicker and dance and, looking deep into those flames, see all sorts of adventures past and future dreams that may work out.

Maybe it's a throwback to hairy figures in primitive caves huddled around a flickering flame on a cold night. I can imagine them glancing fearfully out at the darkness. They know there are ghosties and ghoulies and beasties who prowl and howl and hide in the shadows, in the darkness beyond that circle of light. The demons will getcha if you don't stay close.

They're right, you know. I, too, am drawn to the fire. I stare into the flickering flames, the yellows, the blues and the orange throbbing coals. Sometimes they're white, pulsating with heat. That ancestor, the brute with the sloping forehead, the dim light of perception barely flickering in its brain, hunched over, knuckles near dragging the ground, he, too stared at the flames and those same throbbing coals. The fire was identical. Since that first creature peered at that strange tongue of dancing flame he probably thought was alive it hasn't changed. Fearful he would have stayed in his hiding place. Maybe it appeared in a flash of lightning in a crash of thunder. Maybe he thought it was some kind of god. It came from nowhere and now leaps and twists and dances entrancingly. It radiates warmth. It gives light. It was a thing to fear. It still is.

In today's home, with a flick of your finger, you move an indicator on a thermostatic control. In another location, locked up in a secure box in your basement, a dormant fire springs to life to generate the heat the controller calls for. Confined and controlled it is an obedient servant. Out of control it is a thing to be feared. It is a destroyer. It's like a captive bear or any wild animal. You may think it's tame, docile, domesticated. It may even do tricks that you've taught it, whatever you wish. Don't be fooled. Take care. It is not tame. It's just not eating you at the moment.

I can look into the fire and see other campfires, other places, other times. I can see my father and I during a hunting season by a huge split rock in the woods where we had stopped to eat our lunch. It wasn't far from that rock I stopped and made a campfire with Lori and Benny, my son and daughter, beside a small stream running through the woods. I remember sailing down the Mississippi River with Dorothy when we camped on a sand bar in the middle of the river beside our small sailboat. There was another night when I was alone with a little campfire beside a pup tent on the desert in Arizona. I see the open fire at a Maori feast while visiting the North Island of New Zealand. And there was a time during the Vietnam War, a small fire beside a river in the jungle of Indo China. And my son, Benny and I in the snow by the Yellow Dog River late one night toasting sandwiches and drinking hot chocolate. All those adventures are right there, right there in that fireplace.

My mother had this house built in 1968. She and my father had collected some of those rocks that she had set into the face of the fireplace. There are a couple pieces of petrified wood, a large piece of quartz I think they found down in Arkansas, a thing called Kona stone, I don't know what else. Mom could look at her fireplace and wander wherever she and Dad had been in the travel trailer they toured with.

The fireplace mantle is a weathered timber that washed up on the shore of Lake Superior. It has holes that appear to have been worn through it - strange and intricate - mysterious. What made them? How were they formed? I suspect it may be a timber from the hull of the sailing ship Siskowit that sunk just offshore back, I would guess, in the 1840s. We'll probably never know. Someone said rocks moved back and forth by water currents made the holes. It would have taken years of waves and water currents working those rocks back and forth to wear holes through that timber. Maybe that's what did it - maybe not. Another mystery in the fireplace, another wonder to puzzle over.

The wind blows outside. Branches thrash about in frustration while sleet rattles against the window. The fireplace flames twist and turn, rise and fall and send shadows dancing across the walls. And the fire warms me – inside and out.

♎

Life is Not a Destination

THE GOLDEN DAYS

There's a little nip in the air mornings. Leaves are changing color. The days of summer are drawing to a close. Snowbirds, both the birds and those folks who go south each fall, are beginning to group together to migrate southward. It's a shame they leave so early. They'll miss the quiet serenity of fall in this land of golden beauty. It's their choice – and their loss.

The dawn comes later and later each morning. Evening twilight is earlier and earlier too. A person no longer has to get up early to enjoy the splendor of sunrise or stay up late to watch the tranquility of sunset. These are the golden days of fall in Upper Michigan.

There's a maple tree on the west side of the bayou in front of our house. That hardy little tree is nestled among a group of pines. During the summer the green of the pine needles and maple leaves blend together and that little maple can be easily overlooked. With the coming of fall however its leaves explode into beautiful bright crimson. Early on a clear morning before the rest of the world comes awake the first rays of a rising sun highlight that little tree in a glorious luminescence. I sit at the kitchen table, coffee in hand and marvel at the quiet splendor. That little maple tree is the queen of the scene. She seems to be overseeing the bayou, reflecting in the still water, ruling and directing the bestowal of fall beauty on the marsh and all that surrounds us.

Closer to the house a flock of ducks have assembled in the water just below the porch. They're waiting for me to feed them. Each morning I scatter a measure of whole corn and a loaf of day-old bread on and into the shallow waters of the bayou. They seem to remember me - or at least remember where they can get breakfast. They are there every morning.

Now and then a mink comes by. I don't know where it came from but it seems to like the neighborhood. I'm guessing the mink has a burrow in the bank beside the water.

Geese drop in now and again too but lately they've been pretty scarce. I've watched them forming up into their "V's," talking to one another as they take flight and head south.

Chipmunks will be holing up for the winter before long. They're still with us for a few more days though. They scurry busily back and forth, cheeks puffed out with sunflower seeds from our bird feeders, hurrying to stow them in their burrow. I heard that folks up in Ishpeming and Negaunee had to clear snow off their cars a couple mornings ago. That means it won't be long 'til the chippies will disappear for the winter and the rest of us will be scraping snow.

Squirrels will be with us all winter as will the crows. Blue Jays, always wary, bounce in, glance furtively right and left, quickly gobble a peanut or two I've scattered on the porch and are gone. An otter swims casually by. A Bald Eagle drifts over the bayou riding thermal currents high in the air. It rarely has to move its wings. It traces a lazy circle in the morning sky and drifts on eastward.

Watching all this I wonder why I don't remember seeing these things when I was a kid? But then again we didn't live on a bayou on Lake Superior's shore. When you're young, and middle age too for that matter, life seems to be a rush to get to - - - to get to where? The Indians, the "Native Americans" would sagely say, "They don't know where the center of the earth is." It isn't 'til you're much older that you come to the realization that life is not a destination. Life is what you do, what you see and what you enjoy along the way. We seldom discuss the "destination" but we all know what it is.

Later that morning while driving to Marquette I am taken by the deep rich blue of Lake Superior. Approaching Marquette's lower harbor the contrast of the dark blue lake with the red ore-stained bulk of the ore dock stands out sharply. The images seem clearer, more distinct than they were during the lazy days of summer.

It seems too that later in the day, when full light arrives, everything loses the sharp clear delineation that's apparent in early morning. Their outlines seem to fade into the blur of appointments and schedules and the preoccupation of the day. The streets and the highway are quiet and still at this early hour. It seems it's their "break time" as they patiently await the surge of traffic that's maybe a half hour or so away.

A new day is here and we'll all soon be caught up in the hustle and bustle of schedules and meetings and appointments that are our daily lives. But these moments are mine alone.

I wonder if the "Donut Hole" will be open yet? A second cup of coffee sounds pretty good about now – and maybe a fresh donut while I chew on all these thoughts.

Ω

LOST

This happened to me – oh – it must have been back in the 1940s. I was in my teen years – early teen years. One of those experiences that help convince a kid that he just might not yet know everything about everything.

The morning started out cold, chilly. The woods were beautiful. Here and there was a tree that stood out - pure gold - or bright red. The early sun brought out the colors in bold relief against the shadows behind. The tall grass, covered with frost, sparkled like diamonds. How fortunate we are to live in a land like this.

Maybe you're hunting. Maybe you're just out for a walk. Whatever the reason this part of the world is sedate, calm, and beautiful. Just below the bank the Yellow Dog River flows by on its way to - wherever rivers go. You can hear it roiling as it passes over a fallen log, tumbling all over itself. It digs a deep hole where trout can hide in the shadows out of the main current. The river changes, a bank washes out, a tree falls across - into - the current and the course gradually moves, but the river goes on. I wonder how many years - ages - eons - that river has flowed by here? I hope it continues.

My Dad brought me here. I brought my son. I brought my grandsons. The grandsons are from Texas - they'd never seen anything like this. I showed them how to use a compass, where the roads and rivers and hills were. Away they went, through the woods, with grandpa more scared for them than they were. You gotta do what you gotta do.

I got lost up here one time - well - not really "lost," but I was confused for several hours. I was young and was "at the deer huntin' camp" with the men.

I'd gone out with my dad and a couple of the guys. I got separated - took a left instead of a right, I guess,. I evidently wound up behind a hill I hadn't expected to be there.

I wandered around for a couple hours not wanting to admit to myself that I was "lost." At the same time I fully realized I didn't know which way I should go and all my walking was not doing any good.

It began to get dark. My concern about the time and the growing darkness was growing. Are you reading all this? I was getting scared!

I wasn't running – yet - but my footprints were getting noticeably further apart. Luckily - and it was pure luck - I climbed a hill to try to get a look around. From a bare rock outcrop I saw a lamp light in a window down in the valley. Whoop-dee-doo!

I came down that hill like an avalanche. As I drew near the lighted cabin window I recognized it as a neighbor's hunting camp about two miles from our cabin. I <u>knew</u> where I was!

Suddenly the woods, the hills, the whole world looked friendlier - even in the growing gloom and darkness.

I didn't take the "direct" route through the woods but I high tailed it down a couple logging roads I knew. I was headed back to camp.

It was full dark when I arrived. Some of the men were there but not dad and those with whom I'd gone out. I quietly walked in and got a cup of coffee as if everything was just the way I'd planned it. No one paid any particular mind to me for which I was thankful. I sure wasn't going to say anything.

It was only a few minutes later that the headlights of a car came racing up the old logging road to the cabin. The headlights flashed wildly this way and that as the car bounced and ricocheted off the bumps and ruts that were the road. It slid to a stop in front of the cabin.

The door burst open and my father rushed in. He stopped dead in his tracks when he saw me. There was dead silence all around for several seconds.

"Oh! You're here," he said

I nodded sheepishly.

"I'll go back up to the slashing and get Gordon and Carl. You wanna come along?"

I recognized the look and the tone. It said, "You wanna come along," but it meant, "You! Out in the car!" It was one of those things we all learn to read. It was phrased like a question but it was a command.

Dad drove more slowly, more carefully, on the way to pick up the others. All was silence for the first few minutes. I sure wasn't going to say anything.

Finally he threw a sidelong glance my way and asked, "Where didja go?"

I shrugged my shoulders, a little afraid of what might be next.. "I dunno. I came out down by Hultgrens."

He didn't say anything, just nodded. "Gordon and Carl are keeping a big fire going on the rise where we parked the car."

I didn't say anything.

"We thought you might have got lost, thought you might see the fire and come to it."

"Well, Dad, I guess I did get lost. I'm sorry."

"It's all right, son. It's all part of the woods. There are woodsmen who have been lost and woodsmen who will be lost. There isn't any other kind."

That sure sounded good to me. After another brief few moments I managed to say, "I guess I'd better thank the guys for tending the fire."

In the reflected light from the instrument panel I thought I detected a slight smile, a private thing. He nodded and said, "That'd be nice."

I expected to get a ragging from the guys about getting lost but, you know, nobody said any more about it. Nobody! It was my first "lost." I guess you're allowed at least one.

♎

"Whom shall we send . . .
who will go for us?
Here am I. Send me."
Book of Isaiah, chap 6, verse 8

WHOM WE SEND IN HARM'S WAY

Got a letter the other day. Well, it wasn't so much a letter as a short note. It was from an old friend whom I hadn't heard from for some time. It seems her grandson; nineteen years old, not long out of high school had joined the United States Marine Corps. He completed basic training and had been sent in harm's way to Iraq.

The young fella is an outdoorsman. He had spent some of his time up in the Yellow Dog Plains area, an area with which I too am familiar. Anyway Grandma laid the sweet-talk on me with a trowel praising my

181

writing ability, my books and "just love" my newspaper columns. The hook to all this was would I write "a note" to her grandson. It would be a "support the troops" thing. Being a veteran of the Korea and Viet Nam War I was very aware of the importance of the support the troops in the field receive from the folks back home. Yes, ma'am, I will.

It's important to everyone but particularly to these kids and you have to know that a lot of our soldiers, sailors and airmen are still kids. They suddenly find themselves far away from home for the first time in their lives. They're in a strange land. The customs are different. People wear different clothing.

In a strange land you may find that you have offended someone without realizing it. A fella can't understand the language. And then a couple of them laugh. A young fella with an as yet fragile self-image may feel they're laughing at him. It generates a feeling of isolation although the truth is that they're probably not thinking of him at all. On the parade grounds with fellow soldiers there's a feeling of unity, of invincibility. The solitary hours of a long and lonely night are something else.

Will I write her grandson a note? Yes I will. I'll send him a copy of a book I've written about the Yellow Dog area. We've got things in common, he and I, not only roaming the Yellow Dog plains but serving in the armed forces, being a stranger in a foreign land. It's reaching out to a fella who's a long way from home and letting him know he's not alone.

A couple days later another surprise came. This one was in the form of an e-mail: "...talking to my cousin's wife...you know her mother... (her) son...over in Iraq... the son is my dad's nephew." The sender and her dad were good friends of mine. I didn't know of the connection to this young marine. As she said when ending her note, "small world."

And the world is small and getting smaller. Somebody once said each of us is only six persons removed from knowing everyone in the world. The person you know knows someone you don't know who knows someone and so on. I'm not sure of the numbers or the mathematics but you get the idea. It's something to think about.

We're all closely connected with one another whether we realize it or not. With today's communication and transportation the world has shrunk. The worldwide internet is shrinking it further every day. Are we our brother's keeper? Well, I don't know about "keeper" but we are fast becoming brothers and sisters – and there are differences of opinion in the family. If we can't somehow learn to live peaceably with one another we're in serious danger of destroying ourselves. Those we elect or accept as the statesmen of our world have the heavy responsibility of resolving these differences. Our young marine along with the rest of our military can buy us time but answers to global questions are necessary. Until the answers are found we will continue to send young men and women, the cream of our society and the hope of our future, into harm's way. We are all brothers and sisters, we're brothers and sisters to each of them. John Donne, a seventeenth century English poet and preacher, stated it well: "No man is an island . . . any man's death diminishes me because I am involved in mankind. And therefore never send to know for whom the bell tolls; it tolls for thee."

We Americans send our soldiers and sailors forth in what we see as noble undertakings. The powers that control such things work hard to find solutions to complex problems. We folks back home are proud of and support each and every one of you. So, young marine keep your chin up and your head down. We're thinking of you every day and are waiting to welcome you back home.

Ω

"You're a grand old flag,
you're a high flying flag;
And forever, in peace, may you wave.
You're the emblem of the land I love,
The home of the free and the brave."

George M. Cohan

THE TWINS

A bell.

A ringing bell.

Why is a bell ringing?

Black! Dark! The bell keeps ringing.

The phone! The phone is ringing in the dark. I grope across the bed, clumsily, toward the sound. The alarm clock clatters to the floor.

Damn!

The dial lights up as the handset falls off the carrier. I manage to retrieve it and get it to my ear.

"Hello?"

"Ben! Can you come out and fly?"

"What? To - to do - where? Whassa matter?"

"There's a couple babies, born prematurely, down in Iron River. The hospital called. If they don't get them to Marquette they don't think they'll make it."

"Yeah! Well - - yeah! Have you checked the weather? Iron River? That little strip on top of the hill?"

"Yeah. The weather is OK here and they think it's OK down there but there's no report from there, you know. Can you come out and look?"

"Yeah. I'll be right out."

"The doctor is on the way out too. He's bringing incubators and stuff he says they'll need."

The doctor's on the way out, he says. Bob was

evidently pretty sure of me. "OK. I'll be right out."

"I'll get the airplane ready."

"OK."

The dial light goes out as I replace the phone.

I lay back on the pillow for a moment, blink my eyes real hard and try to sort out what has just happened. Bob Shimaneck and Emil Kaurala own and operate Northern Airmotive, a flight operation at our local airport. I fly airplanes - any kind someone doesn't keep me away from - at any time. I love to fly. So they call me. They call mostly on weekends or during bad weather or at night - night! What time is it?

Fumble for the light, look at my watch: 1:00 AM. Problems! Two babies! Kids! Why is it with kids it's always at night?

Geeezus! At Iron River, too! There's just that little narrow strip on top of the hill out there. I wonder if the runway lights are working? Sometimes, in those little backwoods strips, they don't get around to fixin' all the things that need fixin'.

I wonder if anyone has plowed the snow off of what runway there is? Well, it would appear we're about to find out.

I dress warm. It's December in Upper Michigan. There's snow everywhere and the frost goblins are out there waiting to bite you wherever they can. The cabin heater in the plane isn't anything to write home about either.

I pop a cup of water in the microwave. Instant coffee

is the only thing hot I'll get for quite a while. I'll drink it as I drive up to the airport.

My flight kit is in the car - not all the charts and things, just my personal gear. Balance the coffee cup, slide behind the wheel, start the engine - ah - all went well. I ease the car out the drive, onto the road, and gently guide it down the highway. It's been snowing, the roads are slippery, and, besides, I don't want to spill my coffee.

I wonder how Northern Airmotive happened to get this call? A couple doctors from the local hospital bought out Northern's competitor at the field and have been handling almost all the "Lifeguard Flights," the air ambulance, ever since. The rumor is that the investment is a tax shelter thing. Anyway, they seem to have the inside track on the gravy flights - good weather, first line airports, and well-insured patients.

Bob and Emil get the rest. "Send (us) your poor, your huddled masses, yearning . . ." for a little help - and the boys "lift their lamp . . ." They don't turn away someone in need. I guess that's why I always come when they call. Who knows? Maybe we'll get to heaven that way? Couldn't hurt.

The few snowflakes coming down aren't really a problem - as long as it doesn't get worse.

Those snowflakes. They catch the headlights, streaking right at you then curve slightly away. It reminds me of the flak we flew through in Southeast Asia. As long as it was curving away you were OK. I think of that every time I drive at night in the snow.

Approaching the county airport, the rotating beacon light sweeps the bases of the low hanging clouds. The windshield wipers slap back and forth, wiping the snow off the windshield. The speedometer clicks rhythmically. In the soft glow of the dashboard lights the speedometer needle bounces slightly. I'll have to fix that one of these days.

The floodlights are on in front of the hangar. The airplane has been rolled out. The ambulance is there, lights flashing, beacons rotating. Ambulance "adrenaline" must be coursing through its fuel lines.

The flight service station is quiet at this hour. The dispatcher is on duty though, 24 hours a day. Local weather indicates a 200-foot cloud layer, scattered clouds, with a higher layer - 2,000 feet - solid overcast. Visibility is good. Ground temperature is 18 degrees, winds from the northwest at 12 knots with gusts to 18. Cloud ceilings are lower to the west and the whole mess is moving this way. Welcome to the real world.

"How's Iron River," I ask?

The dispatcher doesn't answer, just turns his head and looks over the rim of his glasses at me.

"OK." I shrug my shoulders. Iron River doesn't report weather. "So how's Iron Mountain?"

Iron Mountain is about thirty miles southeast of Iron River. It has published instrument approaches and reports the weather. Iron River - well - I just hope somebody's plowed the runway - if I can find the runway.

We discuss the weather system a bit, speculate, wonder and guess. I elect to take a shot at it. I'll file a flight plan to Iron Mountain, all nice and legal and all, but I'll try to slip underneath, divert to Iron River. There's a coupla little girls over there that evidently need us pretty badly.

As I walk back toward the hangar I think of the guys in the flight service station. I don't know if I've told them lately but I sure do appreciate them. There's a big, thick book somewhere that tells them the things they have to do - the regulations - but these guys are always willing to go the extra mile. Not necessarily the reception one finds dealing with governmental agencies. Ah, but guys don't say things like that to other guys - not usually. It sure would be nice if we did. I approach the hangar, flight kit in hand.

Bob sees me coming and slips out the door to meet me.

"Ben we've got a problem. How many seats do you need?"

I look at him close. He's worried. "How many people are there, Bob?"

"Well, there's the doctor and three nurses but they've got two incubators with power packs and the rest of the medical gear they say they've got to take along."

Bob already knew the answers to these questions. We look at each other in silence. I look at the little twin engine Aztec airplane and then back at Bob. "I think we can forget about the seats."

"What do you mean?"

"Bob, there's not enough room for those four and the incubators and all that other gear if we put anything in there but my seat."

"Can we do that?"

"Are you asking 'can we' or are you asking 'may we'?"

Bob just stood and looked at me. There are rules - and there are rules - and there are two little girls in Iron River. "I'm asking what you want to do?"

Good ole' Bob. When the goin' gets tough - well - it's nice to have guys like Bob around. We both want to get those two little girls to the hospital at Marquette, to give them a fighting chance to get to know their parents - maybe.

"Take everything but the pilot's seat out. Get all the stuff aboard and we'll go."

I arrange my gear in the cockpit. Bob waves the medical people out and they help load their equipment in the airplane. Those incubators take up a lot of space. When Mr. Piper designed the Aztec I don't think he had this sort of loading in mind.

"Doctor, do the folks in Iron River know you're coming?" That might sound foolish on the face of it but I've been down this road before. Better to ask.

"I talked to them before we left the hospital. They'll be waiting at the airport." He glances at his watch, cocks his head to see it in the floodlight. "They're probably there now."

We all climb into the aircraft. The doctor and nurses

arrange themselves in whatever space is available around the incubators and the power packs and - well - they get in there somewhere.

"Have you folks got everything you're going to need? I'll do what's necessary to get you there and back but you'll have to take care of all the pulse counting and such."

There's a little chuckle that kind of eases the tension. They're a gutsy bunch too. "We've got everything we need."

"Has everyone here flown with Northern Airmotive before? In this airplane?"

They nod affirmatively in the dim light.

"Well, here are the door handles." I indicate the levers. "This trip you're not going to have a seat. Find a secure place, put a strap around you if you can, and just hang on."

Nods and mumbles of assent and all is quiet.

Outside, by the left wing tip, Bob stands watching us.

I raise my left hand, index finger extended, and twirl it in the traditional signal for engine start.

Bob nods, indicating that the propeller area is clear and all is ready.

The engine coughs out a lungful of smoke, barks once or twice, and settles into a low rumble. The right engine next. Check the gauges, the instruments, the warning lights, the radios. I trace down the checklist carefully. If something isn't working properly, this is the time and place to discover it. We're going to need all the help we can get tonight.

"Marquette Radio, Lifeguard flight 6625 Yankee taxiing out for departure, instruments to Iron Mountain."

"Roger, '25 yankee. Winds are from three zero zero degrees at one zero gusting to one eight favoring runway two six. Altimeter two-niner-one-zero. Clearance is on request." I'm the only one that hears this - through the headset. The airplane is silent under the rumble of the engines.

I taxi out very slowly and carefully. It's icy and, if the brakes are used too much they will generate heat, snow will melt on them, freeze, and the next time we touch down we'll be a toboggan.

There's a short break in the sequence of checks and I glance back at my passengers. They sit quietly in their crowded quarters. Pretty gutsy, out here in the ice and snow to do whatever is necessary to get the job done. People like that are getting to be a rare breed. We need to appreciate them more.

My earphones crackle as the flight service attendant keys his microphone. Here comes our air traffic control clearance. ". . . Air traffic control clears lifeguard flight six six two five yankee to . . ."

I read the clearance back to insure there have been no misunderstandings. We are cleared for take off. I taxi onto the runway.

"Weather is the same, 'two five yankee. Have a good flight."

"Roger, Marquette, thank you." I grin to myself in the darkness. Marquette radio is doing all it can to help too. The extra mile.

I turn back toward my passengers. "We're ready to go, folks. Everything OK?"

Heads nod. The doctor says, "OK."

Throttles ease forward to full power. The two Lycoming engines surge forward against their mounts, growling, challenging anything to hold them back.

A quick final check of the engine instruments under full power as the flight controls come alive. We gently lift off the icy runway. The plane is in its element and responds to my gentle pressures on the controls.

Again routine procedures occupy me. The airplane responds smoothly, navigation lights blinking off and on as they should. I ease the engines back from their "maximum effort" and we all settle into the extended flight mode.

K.I. Sawyer Air Force Base Radar monitors us as we leave Marquette. They turn us over to Minneapolis Center where I obtain a "cruise clearance." This will allow me, within limits, to see if I can find my way to Iron River. For now we drone on toward our filed destination, Iron Mountain.

It's black-dark outside. The wing tip lights reflect their blinking red and green as we slip through the clouds. We are alone in a dimly lit cabin with the drone of our engines.

I check my watch for time flown. I'll estimate our

position, deciding when - and if - we will attempt to divert toward Iron River. We descend slowly, hoping to see something - lights on the ground - anything - before we reach the minimum flight altitude for operations under instrument conditions.

The panel lights glow dimly. I turn them down even more. Night vision comes from the cones, the nerves that provide peripheral vision. Lower light levels, especially red light, allow the iris of the eye to open to enhance "night vision."

There! A light! A light on the ground! Some farmer left his yard light on. Thank you, sir.

Another light! A car going down the road.

All right!

Turn west. Check the watch. In about six minutes we should be over Iron River - and land - if they've got a rotating beacon on so we can locate the airport - if the runway lights are on, even just a few - if they plowed the runway - if we're lucky.

The weather is holding for us. We can't let down among the "snow capped mountains" because we can't see them. We've got to stay up here 'til we can positively locate the airport.

There's another light - a flashing light. It's not the airport beacon though. The airport beacon would be flashing an alternate white and green. This light's red. A red flashing light indicates a closed airport. No, Lord! Not this far and then - wait! Wait! It's the beacon, the rotating beacon on the ambulance. They're waiting at the airport and they've got their lights on.

God? Are you playing games with me? Thank you anyway.

Circling, I can make out runway lights, a few, here and there. Now we let down, slowly, cautiously, lower, circling the airport. Landing gear down – and locked. The runway is two thousand feet long but it's - who knows? - probably very slippery - and we're heavy - and we'll be traveling at about 85 miles per hour.

I make a long, slow turn onto the final approach. There's snow on the runway - the landing lights pick it up. An unbroken field of white - a runway light here and there. That'll be a plus - if it isn't too deep. It'll help slow us down. I hope it's not so deep it'll prevent us taking off again.

As we get closer it begins to rush by faster and faster. Easy now! Eeeeasy! Full flaps. Nose high; touch down as slowly as possible. Stay between the few runway lights I can see.

We're down! Softly. Gently. Keep the nose up for maximum "aerodynamic" braking. Gently, gently, we're on ice. This is the time for friendly persuasion and body english. Keep off the brakes as much as possible. Yeah! All right!

At a slow walk we taxi back along our tracks, back up the runway, onto the ramp, and park beside the ambulance - with its beautiful flashing beacon. Swing the nose into the wind - angle it slightly to protect the entry door. Shut down the engines. The silence is deafening.

The ambulance turns on its side floodlights.

The medical team climbs out. They hurry to the idling ambulance.

I secure the airplane, switches off, tie the controls against the gusting wind. Getting out, I turn up my collar, hunch my shoulders against the cold wind, and seek shelter behind the bulk of the ambulance.

There's a serious discussion going on inside. I shiver a little and wait in the lee of the vehicle, out of the wind.

The babies are still in the hospital in Iron River.

We transfer the equipment from the airplane to the ambulance.

"Any idea when you'll be back, doctor?"

He just shakes his head.

"I'll keep the plane warm and ready." We look briefly at one another. "Whenever."

He climbs into the ambulance, closes the door. With lights flashing and beacon rotating they drive away.

I watch the lights disappear as the sounds fade away. The wind whips across the ramp sending a flurry of snow up the leg of my pants. A dim light shines in a pay phone booth beside the dark airport hangar. The rest of the world is a snow-blown black.

The phone booth is one of those that are open at the bottom. Not much protection there. And the phone doesn't work. The outline of the airplane shows dimly about fifty yards away.

This may be a long night.

The plane rocks gently as I nudge each wing tip with my shoulder. Good! The brakes haven't frozen.

I reach into each engine nacelle, holding my bare hand to feel for any radiant heat. They're not cold - yet - but I don't want them to get cold either. When we next need them there'll be two little girls who'll be counting on them. The light snow seems to be blowing off the aircraft as fast as it comes down. Our tracks are filling in. I'll check the engines again in - let's see - in fifteen minutes. I would guess that starting them every thirty minutes, running them for a few minutes each time, would keep them warm and ready. The cabin heater may even keep me a little warm, too.

Inside the airplane the wind isn't blowing but the cold has already chilled the air. The words of a popular song run through my mind, ". . . those icy fingers up and down my spine, that same old feeling . . ." That ought to be the theme song for charter pilots in winter.

I turn on the battery and turn on a radio. If I don't close out our flight plan, when the stated time runs out a search will be initiated. I have no hope of talking to the center from the ground but am able to raise an airliner high overhead. They relay the message and pass me the closing. If the phone had been working - well - there are a lot of "ifs" in this business. Shut everything down again.

Rummaging in my flight kit I find a book, "Jack Anderson - The Anderson Papers." Not necessarily a best seller but better than staring out at the snow and dark. Gloves to keep the hands warm, a flashlight to see - not the Ritz but better than nothing.

Time drags on.

We landed about quarter to three. At three fifteen I start the engines, run them for five minutes (cabin heater for five minutes), shut them down and go back to the book. I hope the engines got warmer than I did.

At quarter to four I crawl out and inspect the airplane, move each control surface, nudge the wings to re-check the brakes, check for any accumulation of snow.

All's well.

I look down the road leading from the airport - as much as I can see - staring into the darkness.

Nothing! Come onnnn, Doc! It's cold out here.

Back inside the aircraft I start the engines for their "warm up" run. It's cold in here, too.

I intend no criticism but "The Anderson Papers" just aren't grabbing me. Maybe it's the cold and the flashlight and all.

I start the engines at four fifteen and again at quarter to five. It's still black, "inside-of-a-cow" dark.

About five o'clock or shortly thereafter the lights of the ambulance approach down the road.

What took them so long? Maybe they could have driven them to Marquette? Maybe maybe maybe. This is not the time for "maybe."

The ambulance eases up beside the airplane and turns on its lights. I jump out, open the cargo door for the incubator loading, and move to the ambulance to help.

There's a quiet intensity to everyone involved. No light conversation. No joking. Anything that's said is something that needs to be said. All attention is directed to the two incubators and their cargo.

As soon as the incubators are inside the plane the doctor and the nurses follow.

The plane is ready. It has been ready for two and a half hours now. I crawl in last.

The engines start without hesitation, God love 'em, and we move toward the runway.

"Sorry it took so long."

I glance back and see the doctor's face, tired and concerned.

"We had to stabilize them before we dared to move them."

I just nod silently, pass a "thumbs up" signal to indicate all is well, and concentrate on getting us ready to fly. Nice guy. He was concerned about me, the hired help. I wonder if he's really a member of the AMA? Maybe he just missed the course, "Arrogance 101," that so many doctors seem to have passed with flying colors. Well, no time for that now.

The snow has obliterated all signs of our arrival. I find the runway and taxi the full length so we'll have tracks to follow on take-off. I know that "time is of the essence" but this is necessary.

Slowly! Gently! It's still a very icy runway. Don't use the brakes over much.

The ambulance stays parked on the ramp, waiting for us to depart, their red beacon flashing boldly in the night. We hadn't talked about that but I'm glad they stayed.

The flaps are set and all is ready for take-off. Power up on the left engine to turn around. Bring the power up on the right engine as we line up. The landing light illuminates our tracks in the snow. The snow is beginning to drift into them already.

The muttering of the engines rises to a crescendo. Propellers slash the air, pulling us down the runway ever faster. They drag the snow-harried airplane - and us - up and away from the dark, snow covered field. We're in the air again.

Leave the landing gear down for a bit - clear any blown snow away from the up-lock mechanism.

With the airplane smoothly under way I glance back at my passengers. The dim light emanating from the incubators reflects on four intent faces. They are fixed resolutely on those incubators and their cargo - like they were the most precious thing in the world. Tonight, they are.

I cycle the landing gear - up - then down - then up again. We sure don't want the up locks to freeze in the up position. I make the necessary adjustments and the airplane settles to a steady drone. We're heading toward home.

It's somewhat of a farce to try to convince anyone that flying at night in any sort of weather is done visually. Legally, that is what I must claim - at least 'til I am able to contact KI Sawyer AFB approach control. With their radar, they'll be able to furnish the necessary clearances. In the meantime I simply try to avoid the altitudes and/or courses any other airplanes might be following. At this hour of the morning - well - it's a big sky. There's no radio traffic on center frequency.

About ten minutes after take off the amber indicator light of our radar beacon - the transponder - suddenly comes to life. Sawyer's radar is sweeping over our aircraft. I switch to their radio frequency.

"Sawyer, lifeguard six six two five yankee."

Silence. Sawyer probably wasn't expecting anyone at this hour of the morning. As I am about to call again my headset comes alive with the familiar crackle of a signal - someone out there keying a microphone button.

"Aaah, calling Sawyer approach control, say again?"

They're not asleep. Maybe a cup of coffee, but not sleeping.

"Sawyer approach control, lifeguard six six two five yankee."

"Roger, two five yankee, squawk one four zero zero and ident."

I set the figures into our transponder.

"Radar contact, two five yankee. You are forty three miles southwest of Marquette. Turn to zero six zero degrees, maintain three six hundred feet. This is a vector to final approach, runway two six, Marquette County Airport."

"Roger Sawyer." It's all downhill from here.

I switch to Marquette flight service frequency, give them our time of arrival - fifteen minutes - and ask if they will please contact Marquette General Hospital for an ambulance.

"Roger, two five yankee." (The "extra mile" again.) Some places aren't eager to help, even air ambulance flights. I guess the lawyers - and the writers of regulations (I guess they're lawyers, too) - have everyone fearful of liability law suits. Those guys at Marquette have never turned me down though. Maybe I should say something to them? Aaaw! "Guys" don't do that.

My passengers continue to focus full attention on the incubators.

"Doctor, we'll be down in eleven minutes. The ambulance is on its way."

He nods, concentrating on an oscilloscope, its dim green light reflecting on his face.

We break out of the weather while on a slow descent toward the runway. The flashing lights of an ambulance are visible turning in the airport gate. Things are working out well.

The landing and parking are routine.

People swarm over the airplane and our precious cargo. The transfer is quick and efficient. No time is wasted. Ambulance doors slam. Their red rotating beacon swiftly moves away toward the highway. The distant wail of the siren, clearing what little traffic there is at this hour, is the last contact I have.

The snow has stopped. It's still cold. There's a night light on in the Northern Airmotive office. It casts an outline of the window on the snow-covered ramp. The lights of the flight service station are bright in the distance.

I climb back inside the rapidly cooling airplane, secure the flight controls, all switches off, gather my flight kit, and climb out. Door closed. Wheels chocked. I slip the written report of the flight under the door for Vicki to do the billing.

It's about six o'clock - give or take. I'm too tired to look at my watch. Not yet a hint of light on the eastern horizon. Suddenly I am tired - very tired. The flight kit hangs heavy on my arm. The playful wind once more sends a cold gust up my pant leg. I have to smile. Slowly I trudge across the snowy ramp toward my parked car. I brush the snow off the windshield.

I sure hope those little girls make it.

Oh! Yeah! I earned twelve dollars on the current pay scale tonight - if we get paid at all. Another smile. Oh, yeah! We've been "paid" already.

ADDENDUM

The doctor called me six weeks or so later. Unfortunately one of the little girls didn't make it. Something about the premature, something didn't develop sufficiently and burst - something like that. The other made it through the valley of the shadow. She was to be released, to go home with her parents to Iron River. Would I like to come by and see her? Would I!

You bet your stethoscope I would.

I got to the hospital before the parents arrived. Probably just as well. They've had enough complications without me getting in their way. They let me hold that little girl - a gown on and I had to wear one of those mask things. A nurse took our picture - a Polaroid - and gave it to me. It hangs on my wall - over all the military medals and such.

That was darn nice of that doctor. I wonder if he belongs to - ah, well, no matter.

Her name is Bonnie. She doesn't know me but I know her. Her name is Bonnie.

ADDITIONAL ADDENDUM

A local newspaper published this story – oh, it must have been about September 2003 (this expedition took place back about 1972).

A woman in the Western Upper Peninsula of Michigan got 'hold of me: "Did that flight . . . " "Was that involving . . ." "I have a cousin who was born . . ." "She lives over in . . ."

Guess what! We were able to get in contact, Bonnie and I. We exchange Christmas cards and such. She's living over around the Amasa, Michigan area and has invited me to stop by.

I've gotta get by Amasa and see my little girl.

Her name is Bonnie – and she does know me.

Ω

INDEPENDENCE DAY

Independence Day! The Declaration of Independence! "We hold these truths . . .that all . . . are created equal, . . . endowed . . ." but this is not entirely true. 'Most of us probably don't really understand the legal niceties of the "Bill of Rights." We take these "rights," as we understand them, for granted. We don't give much thought to the "big picture," the soldiers, sailors, airmen, marines, coastguardsmen, firemen, police, bank regulators and the whole of our governmental system that makes our lives what they are. We have social security, Medicare, veteran's homes, nursing homes and the list goes on through many social support programs. Never mind that some of them don't seem to function as well as advertised. You don't have to look far to see that a majority of the citizens in the rest of the world are without many "rights," without help, impoverished, are having great difficulty just keeping body and soul together. Many of those less fortunate folks don't make it. Looking at it that way our cup is "half full," not "half empty." Remember your many fellow citizens who make our lives as free as it is every day and be thankful not only on Independence Day.

But that's not really what I want to talk about. I want to address not only independence but to get more specific and talk about some other "rights" that most of us have and take to be "self-evident" also.

Think, if you will, how many of our fellow citizens are not able to function as freely as you and I. "Discrimination," you cry! "Affirmative action" you espouse. "Typical capitalistic exploitation of the proletariat!" (if you're socialistically inclined). We are trying to do something about that but these people aren't discriminated against by race, creed, color or nationality. Their case is special. I'll tell you where you can see it first hand. What's being done will inspire you.

If you're able some Independence Day go up to Big Bay, just north of Marquette, Michigan. Watch members of Bay Cliff Health Camp "marching" in the Fourth of July Parade up there. You'll see a quiet but very real battle being waged here and now for Independence - by children. They're fighting for a degree of freedom from the effects of malnutrition, from catastrophic diseases, from bent and twisted limbs from any of numerous disabilities. These kids, through no fault of their own, suffer these hardships.

The struggle has been going on at Bay Cliff since 1934. That was the year when two courageous women, Goldie Corneliuson and Elba Morse planted their banner on a bluff overlooking Lake Superior and declared war "on anything at all that dims the light in children's eyes."

It was also during the era of the Great Depression. One in every four workers couldn't find a job. Those who were working were not earning enough to write home about. The "light" was pretty "dim" in everybody's eyes back then. I can describe those times to you but real appreciation comes only from having lived it. These days it's only appreciated by those of us with silver hair, who may go to bed with their teeth in a glass and who make several trips to the bathroom each night. Things were bad.

Those two ladies who started Bay Cliff were medical people, a nurse and a doctor. They had been seeing children day after day who, among other ailments, were simply not getting enough to eat. They set out to correct that situation as best they could. It helps to understand the actions of people like that if we recall a bible verse; Isaiah, chapter 6, verse 8. (If that's not exactly right, it's close.) "Whom shall we send and who will go for us? Here am I. Send me." If this is religious, it's religion you can see, touch, taste, feel, not just listen to.

It wasn't a profit-motivated venture, not in the usual sense. This involved giving to your fellow man (and woman). It was charity. Charity is neither a bad nor a demeaning word. "This that we're doing is worthwhile and I believe strongly enough that I ask you to help." Their premise at the start was, "It is better to light a solitary candle than to stand and curse in the dark!"

High on that bluff in Big Bay overlooking Lake Superior they established present day Bay Cliff Health Camp. They reached out to those who weren't able to help themselves, to the children of the depression. Here these two ladies would fight for "these truths we take to be self-evident" for a freedom for these disadvantaged kids. It's been a long and hard uphill struggle. Are you wondering how well they did? Go up to Big Bay. Stop in at Bay Cliff Health Camp. Take a look for yourself.

The day-to-day operation of Bay Cliff is not a showy thing. There's not a lot of publicity or advertising but they have much quiet assistance and support. "The Telephone Pioneers," a group of retired telephone workers, their husbands and wives, quietly donate time and efforts to maintaining the facility. A local motorcycle club, The Superior Chapter of the Harley (Davidson) Owners Group, "HOGs," sponsors an annual fundraiser the proceeds of which are donated to Bay Cliff. Help comes from many businesses and professional people, some with public announcement, some without. More help is always welcomed for the need is growing. Bay Cliff continues to reach out to those not able to reach out themselves.

There are camp counselors who return year after year to help with the children. If you ask them why, they're embarrassed to answer unless they know you and believe you'll understand. It's not the money that attracts them – it's the kids. The spirit, the courage, the determination of those kids is an inspiration to all who witness it. They'll unashamedly tell you those kids give them more than they can ever give back.

There are volunteer medical personnel, specialists working for minimal or no charge. Whatever it takes is what gets done and it's all for the kids. Bay Cliff has always been for the kids. The love that surrounds them up there is all wool and a mile wide. Miracles come in all sizes and varieties and at times and in ways you just don't understand. But they happen. They happen at Bay Cliff Health Camp, a place "where dreams come true" - for those kids.

The Bay Cliff Board of Directors including Camp Supervisor Tim Bennett and his capable staff have launched a program of expansion. They want to open their doors year 'round – for the kids. The expansion will cost an estimated $7,000,000. If past accomplishments are any indication there's not much doubt that they'll do it. The spirit and determination of Doctor Goldie Corneliuson and Nurse Elba Morse is alive and well at Bay Cliff Health Camp.

If you're ever up that way and don't think you'll have an opportunity to visit Bay Cliff, make the opportunity. Stop by Big Bay and visit Bay Cliff Health Camp. If you can make it on Fourth of July you'll not regret it. You'll have the opportunity to watch those kids, those Bay Cliff kids as they pass by in the parade. They'll be wearing costumes they have made themselves. They'll be riding on or pulling floats they've created themselves. Some of them may be pulling each other but they'll all be there. You should particularly notice the light in their eyes as you applaud - applaud 'til your hands are raw. It's a new experience for them – strangers paying attention to them and what they are able to accomplish.

Your applause is a salute to the courage, the tenacity, the determination displayed by handicapped kids fighting for their Independence, for those "rights" the rest of us take to be self-evident. Come by Big Bay and celebrate– for the kids.

Before I close I want to leave you with a thought. Why do you suppose Doctor Corneliuson and Nurse Morse did this? Why do today's medical specialists volunteer to treat these children? Why did Tim Bennett and his staff choose their jobs? Why do people volunteer to help out and operate the Beacon House Inn in Marquette for patients of Marquette General Hospital and their families? Why is The Children's Museum? How did Harbor House, a shelter for abused women, come about? I don't have enough space to list all the reaching out to one another but I'll bet you can add to this list from your own knowledge. Money is not the motivator for these efforts. If you didn't understand what those camp counselors at Bay Cliff were talking about I don't think I can explain it to you. Maybe this quotation says it even better:

"Only a life lived for others
is a life worthwhile."

Albert Einstein

♎

BEACON HOUSE

Maybe it comes on suddenly, like an auto accident or a lightning strike. Maybe it's slow and insidious, a little ache here or a rash or growth there. Maybe it turns up unexpectedly during a medical check-up when the doctor puts on his (or her) serious expression and says, "We'd better check into that." Your fear quotient immediately rises. In case you didn't realize it, so does your blood pressure. There's a major chemical change that surges through your whole body. This experience can be especially heart wrenching if it involves a child.

Whatever it turns out to be you know that modern

medicine can perform wonders. Skilled medical practitioners and modern technology are often able to work miracles. However it goes your attitude has become very serious and life is suddenly very precious - and miracles these days don't come cheap. Whether you're fully insured, relying on Medicaid or anywhere in between there'll be some digging deep into the pocket to cover the cost of turning water into wine. There will also be the expenses of incidental travel and housing and lost time on the job.

Marquette is blessed with the Marquette General Hospital, a first class medical facility that is growing rapidly and steadily. The larger it grows the wider the scope of ailments they are able to treat and, of course, the more patients who'll arrive for treatment.

Marquette has a variety of fine hotels and motels available for primary caregivers, friends and relatives but these too are expensive. Some establishments used to ease the burden some by honoring "hotel vouchers." Unfortunately that program is no longer available. There is a replacement however, bigger and better.

It began with facilities set aside specifically for visitors to the hospital. People traveling to Marquette for medical care were able to avail themselves of the hospitality offered by "Beacon House" and "Hospitality House," two housing facilities located on West College Avenue. In special instances the hospital also provided "hospitality rooms" for family members of critical-care patients. As the hospital grew the need for housing for these people grew also. In addition to basic physical shelter it was realized that these people were under emotional strain, they were hurting inside, they were psychologically torn and desperately needed something more than just room and board.

In recognition of this need in September of 2001 a nonprofit group titled "Hospitality House, Inc." was formed. It was a group of caring individuals, volunteers from across the Upper Peninsula who established and would meet periodically to oversee the operation. Through their efforts and by enlisting the help and the generosity of many caring individuals and businesses a motel/hotel called the "Village Inn" on North Third Street was purchased. It was conveniently located fairly close to both Marquette General Hospital and the Peninsula Medical Center. It has since been remodeled and transformed into what is now called the "Beacon House," Upper Michigan's Hospitality House.

The Beacon House provides 37 guest rooms with private baths. Facilities include a community kitchen/dining area with multiple individual food storage cabinets. There are three separate but adjacent kitchen work areas complete with stoves, large refrigerators and freezers with counter space for the preparation of meals. There is also a large, comfortable living room area with television. There's a computer room and a separate children's playroom. In addition, recognizing special situations, there is also the "Harbor Light Lounge," set aside especially for patients undergoing radiation/

oncology treatment along with their caregivers. Local volunteers donate their time to make coffee, do odd jobs and be available for anyone who just wants to talk. Other volunteers may provide transportation to and from the medical facilities.

Everything about Beacon House is attuned to making Beacon House a "home away from home" for its visitors. The surroundings are designed to offer emotional support to patients and caregivers. It provides an atmosphere that encourages mutual support among people sharing common tragedies and hardships. What about the cost? We haven't mentioned cost. Neither does anyone else at Beacon House. People offer what they can. Skilled personnel and modern technology at all levels provide the tools for healing the body but it takes hope and love and caring to soothe the soul. These are things that can't be purchased - not at any price. But that oh so necessary support is available at Beacon House and in generous supply.

Now let's talk about the money it takes to provide this caring facility – your money. As you have probably guessed, Beacon House is a nonprofit organization – a charity. Operating the way I just described you can readily see that any "profits" are emotional – another commodity that cannot be purchased.

There's nothing demeaning about the word charity. Many immediately visualize a ragged individual squatting on a sidewalk, hand extended, begging for a handout, something on that order. Yes, in some instances but not always so. There are times when each of us needs a little help – a little "charity." Let me give you another definition of charity: "An act or feeling of benevolence or good will." Where Beacon House is concerned forget that first assumption and emphasize the definition I just stated. If any of you want to experience a "feeling of benevolence or good will," if you feel the urge to help, to reach out to your fellow man or woman, call the Beacon House - or its equivalent in your area. You can join friends and neighbors in "an act or feeling of benevolence (and) good will." If cash is a little short – and sometimes it is – donate your time to help out at whatever you're able to do that might prove useful.

In Marquette you might assist Andy Lempisis in building maintenance – or Jack Anderson with making coffee and washing the dishes – or anybody else who happens to be around at the time. Volunteer to do anything you feel you can – we've all got some talent that can prove useful. If you fit in you'll be appreciated. If there's no need at the moment your offer will still be appreciated.

This could be your opportunity to make a miracle happen – maybe for a child. Believe me, you'll feel better for the effort. It'll sooth your soul.

♎

Life is Not a Destination

.

I feel I should prefix this next chapter in the same way television programs alert viewers to controversial subject matter: "The following article contains views which those secure in their religious beliefs may find offensive."

This is not intended as "gospel" (no pun intended). It's simply some musings of someone who feels he may be "wandering in the wilderness." If you choose to read on – and as a result become angry with the author, please keep this warning in mind.

"FORGIVE US OUR TRESPASSES"

I'm not a heathen - at least I don't think I am. You've got me squirming a bit there. I go to church now and then. Well - on Christmas and Easter I do - at least on one of them - usually.

It seems that Churches, Synagogues, Temples, Buddhist Shrines, all have their own unique systems or dogma or edicts that structure their ceremonies. They each have rituals that must be adhered to - and "all those others, those 'sinners', will go to hell."

A fella named Omar Khyayam, a Persian rug merchant who lived around the year 1100 AD wrote an epic poem called "The Rubaiyat." One particular verse has always stayed in my mind:

"When I was young I did often frequent
of Doctor and Saint and heard great argument about it

and about but when all was spent,
I came out by the same door where in I went."

I've "frequented" some of those places too. The arguments are still going on. Nothing seems to have changed and, you know, I don't think it ever will.

There's a God - somewhere. Things in nature, in the world, in the universe are too well designed and coordinated to have just happened but, you know what? I don't think there's anyone down here on earth that knows much about Him – or Her.

Unfortunately there are opportunists, promoters who prey on people's gullibility. "Come to me, all ye who labor and are heavy laden . . ." They promise the moon and the stars "if you believe" – and, of course, cross their palm with a few dollars, yen, rubles, whatever. Who is it that really knows?

Many people go to church because, well, because it's the thing to do. And, what the heck, it's only for an hour once a week or so. If what that preacher promises really works everything is gonna be wonderful. And if it doesn't, well, what the heck, it's only for an hour once a week or so.

To many folks I think it's like a lottery ticket. The odds may be – well – the odds aren't important because the payoff is grand beyond comprehension.

I sometimes sense what appears to be a contradiction. Those who are assuring us that heaven is a wonderful and desirable place seem a little uncertain themselves.

When they're not feeling well, when those pearly gates might be swinging open for them, they too are on the first plane to the Mayo Clinic, just like you and me.

When I was a little boy the impression I had of "God" was of a stern looking old man in a long white robe with flowing white hair and beard. He sat on a big throne away high up on top of some stairs. He didn't smile at all. Angels fluttered around above him playing harps. Everybody sang hymns and hosannas (whatever "hosannas" are) and held their hands pressed together like in all the pictures. I saw myself watching all this from where I assumed a "wretch" like me would be seated - away down low among the bugs and the spiders and the mice.

A pipe organ played occasionally, very ponderous funeral-like dirges. And they were telling me this was what heaven was? I would catch myself wondering, you know, if they might not be havin' more fun in that other place. And then I'd be scared because I was also told He knows everything you're thinking.

Here's a story I heard about the experience of a missionary off somewhere "among the heathens." One young fella came to religious services faithfully. He would listen to the word attentively. He sang and rejoiced with the rest but, when the offer was extended to convert, he held back. The missionary had occasion to speak with this lad privately one day and he asked him, "Why don't you join the church, become a Christian?"

The young fella' looked down, scuffed the dirt with

his foot, and finally looked up and said, "Well, I like your stories and I like to sing your songs. Your Jesus Christ is quite wonderful - but you Christians don't seem to be anything like him."

It seems that ceremonies, the rituals, the public "rending of the garments" gives people what they want - a physical "something to do." It provides a satisfaction to the individual. They feel they have "performed" so, quid pro quo, they can expect to be rewarded.

I wonder if that's really what God wants us to do?

The first time I had that thought I was afraid heavenly lightning might flash down and get me. Then I thought, you know, Thomas was with Christ through the crucifixion. But he had his doubts. When the other guys rushed in and said, "Hey! We've seen him! He walked with us along the road." Thomas replied, "Horse hockey! (or an equivalent expression appropriate to that day and time) Unless I see him, put my hand in the wound, etc." you remember the story. If Thomas, who was there all along had questions, I guess I can try to use the brains God gave me to try to figure this out too.

Each religion subscribes to a philosophy centering on love and compassion. All seem to recognize the "Golden Rule," the difference between right and wrong. Why don't we all live that way?

People who gain satisfaction from ceremonies should go on performing them. As long as it doesn't hurt anyone else it ought to be all right.

The same world exists outside a church or synagogue

or mosque or temple. Practice religion outside too. Live what you believe. Don't simply tell people what you are, show them by the way you live. Set a standard, your own standard in your own corner of the world. If others admire and approve of it maybe they'll follow your example. The idea will spread. Then that young fella the missionary was having trouble with might be convinced that we're more like "our Jesus Christ" and join us. Maybe then too we wouldn't feel so desperate about getting someone to "forgive us our trespasses."

♎

"Going to Church doesn't make you a Christian any more than going to the garage makes you an automobile"

Billy Sunday

"*If there are no dogs in Heaven, then when I die, I want to go where they went.*"

-Will Rogers

The Kids

"These things I despise
Hypocrisy — and lies -
And anything at all that dims
The light in children's eyes."

Ruth T. Stomper

Life is Not a Destination

BURIED PIRATE'S TREASURE

Two of our grandchildren go to the beach each summer at Port Aransas, down in Texas, with their parents, my daughter Lori and her husband. The vacation is a too-short two weeks in July but they squeeze a lot of good times into that couple of weeks. Grandma and I had the opportunity to get in on the fun one year. Let me tell you about that summer.

Dorothy (grandma) and I owned a small (25 foot) sloop, "Seaclusion," that we kept at "Pirates Cove," a little marina in Alabama. We thought it might be fun to take it down to Port Aransas for the kid's vacation. Dorothy was working at the time and couldn't arrange time off except for the short vacation at Port Aransas. It was decided that I would go to Pirate's Cove ahead of time and sail "Seaclusion" on an eighteen-day cruise down the Intercoastal Waterway to Port Aransas. Those eighteen days were a fun trip in themselves but that's another story. I'll tell you about it another time, if you're interested.

A few days after I arrived at Port Aransas, grandma, daughter Lori and her husband and grandsons Joshua and Nicky arrived. They came in a motorhome grandma and I used as a vacation home and that I had previously positioned at the kid's house in Fort Worth. With the combined accommodations of the motorhome and the boat we were able to save on a motel bill and we were all able to stay together at the dock in the Port Aransas Marina.

The two boys, six and eight years old at the time, immediately took over Grandpa's Boat. They wanted to steer, they wanted to sail, they wanted to pull tug or tie every rope (line) in sight. They had their momma nervous as a long-tailed cat in a room full of rocking chairs. They crawled all over the afterdeck, the foredeck, the bowsprit, and several places no one had ever crawled before. We fitted them both in life vests and let them have at it.

One day we all got aboard and headed for someplace away from the crowds. In the couple days before they all arrived I had discovered a secluded beach, an out-of-the-way inlet remote and accessible only by water. Aye, matey, we went to places said to have been frequented, "in the olden' days," by pirates! Avast, ye swabs!

At a small bay we anchored just offshore. It was a beautiful spot with shallow water for the boys to swim, wade, chase crabs, and the million other things that little boys do. Everyone wandered around, exploring for shells and pebbles and whatever we turned up. After a bit momma and grandma busied themselves preparing lunch. We had arranged for a genuine "sea-dog" (hot dog) lunch roasted-on-a-stick over an open-fire. Their daddy was trying his hand at fishing, casting in the surf a ways down the beach. Aah, but grandpa, devious grandpa was off by himself conniving a plan.

Prior to arriving at Port Aransas, I had picked up a small wooden jewelry box with brass hinges, a lock, and a hasp. I had also bought a handful of dime-store jewelry, beads and baubles and gotten fifteen or twenty dollars worth of change - pennies, nickels, dimes, quarters, a couple half dollars.

Quietly, unobtrusively, while everyone was occupied with their separate pursuits, I took out my "treasure chest" and its booty. Carefully concealing it from the sight of any casual observer I smuggled it ashore. It was necessary that I first survey the area to select landmarks for a "Treasure Map." The treasure map was, of course, an integral part of "the plan." Lessee, "Start where the knot of sea grass tops the sandy dune, thence go west, toward the settin' sun, blood red in the dyin' light." Well, not exactly "dying" yet, but a little imagination is necessary here - work with me on this. I've got to take care to measure the number of (six and eight year old) paces while eluding the suspicion of anybody that might casually glance my way. "Olden' days" pirates were precise about their map-making you know.

Ah, there's another landmark. I scribble myself a note. "Go 'leventeen paces to that gnarled old tree reachin' bony arms skyward." Hey! I'm really gettin' into this thing.

I came across the picked-clean bones of some bird that had gone to that great seashore in the sky. Gathering the bones I continued searching for another landmark. There! There's another one! "Aaarg, matey, now ye must go to the sou'wards, towards the distant collection of brush and such." Count the paces, smuggle the "loot," keep the bones hidden and avoid suspicion. Lemme tell you, it ain't easy, bein' a pirate.

I stumbled across a broken oar and an old life vest, washed up by the waves. I'm in luck! "Thence three paces to my mark, a busted oar and lifejacket and only the bones that's left of my pore ole shipmate, Jim. Aaargh, Jim, I'll miss ya matey."

I was behind a low dune now and out of sight of everyone. I carefully moved the trash aside and dug a shallow hole in the sand. Placing the treasure chest in the hole I covered it partially then deposited the bones of "poor ole shipmate, Jim" (the seagull) with proper reverence. I covered it all and replaced the "trash." Smoothing the sand to obscure evidence of my being there, I eased away from the scene by another route so as not to be discovered in the area. My hope is that shortly this area will attract a lot of interest.

Returning to "Seaclusion" I go below and dig out an old piece of parchment type paper. Gathering what materials were on hand, I waxed eloquent with a shot at a little calligraphic "pirate type" writing:

Aaargh, Mateys! and this here's the
"TREASURE MAP"
of Peg Leg Pete, the Pirate.

Ye must start by the spot near the shore where the land is sort of pointy-like.

From there go 62 paces straight west, where the sun sets, blood red in the dyin' light o' day. You'll come to a spot where the oyster shells is in a pile - by the gnarly ole tree reachin' scraggly-like to the sky.

Then you must go sou'ward another 40 paces to the little bush growin' all by itself on top of a sand hill - by a brush pile.

Right near that bush is a small hill of sand marked by the broken oar with which I busted me pore ole' shipmate Jim's head.

He helped me dig the hole, don'cha see, and I didn't want no one left to tell the tale. Right there's his life jacket too.

Aargh, he ain't gonna need it no more.

***That's the place where you must dig for
Treasure!***
Good Luck, Matey.
signed:
***PEG LEG PETE, THE PIRATE . (his
mark) "X" (in real blood)***

The map was embellished, of course, with suitable
lines and arrows and "X marks the spot" and skulls and
cross bones and things as best grandpa could do. I would
have drawn a parrot too but my enthusiasm was rapidly
surpassing my abilities.

An empty peanut butter jar was the best I could come
up with. I pressed it into service. The map edges were
tattered, the map folded, and I carefully put it in the jar.
I sealed the lid and once more sneaked ashore.

The boys were absorbed in digging for shells,
splashing in the water, enjoying the day. The bottle
delivery was kind of over-the-shoulder into-the-ripples
near the shore. Grandpa pulled this off in a manner that
would do any spy proud. All the elements were now
in place. I retreated some distance and watched for the
plot to unfold.

The bottle bobbed and jiggled but went unnoticed!
Son of a gun! All that conniving and they weren't even
going to see it? What to do? What to do? I couldn't
say, "Hey! Look! What's that?" without blowing my
cover. The kids are little but they're not stupid. They
know that two and two make four.

I fidget and fret for nearly half an hour before the smallest one, Nicky, noticed the bottle. It had nudged aground and was rolling in the slight ripple of the surf. My breath is coming short now. I'm trying to watch without seeming to look. Will he take the bait?

He looks. He picks up the peanut butter jar and examines it more closely. Darn! I think he's going to throw it back. No! No! He shakes the jar. He sees the paper inside. He struggles with the top. It's too tight! He looks at it again then runs down the beach calling to his brother, Joshua. "Look! Look! Look what I found. There's a paper inside."

Joshua looks at it disdainfully, the way an older brother does when a younger brother has found something he wishes he had found first. "Aw! It's just an old bottle."

"But there's a paper in it. Maybe there's something on the paper? Let's take it to Momma." That's the solution to all the world's problems. Take 'em to momma.

Momma and grandma had a fire going by now and were getting the hot dogs ready for roasting. They listened. They looked. They too had trouble with the jar top. Finally it came off. A letter! A note! Something with writing on it! From where I was hidden I was more excited than the kids were. They're jumping up and down. "What does it say? What does it say?" Grandma began reading the message aloud. Their eyes grew big. This was really something! Peg Leg Pete! A Pirate!

I guessed it might be appropriate to make an entrance

about now. Casual, you know, just sort of wander up. Joshua is into it too now, beyond the big brother little brother thing. "Grandpa! Look! Nicky found a thing from a pirate!"

"It looks like a treasure map," Grandma adds.

"Nicky found a treasure map from a pirate!"

"It was just floatin'. Right over there." Nicky's big eyes are shining as he points excitedly.

I "ooh" and "aaah" as befits one late to learn the details.

"Well, let's read the map," grandma says. "Look! It says to start over there, by the shore."

Grandma catches my eye with a sidelong knowing glance. I shrug innocently.

The boys don't notice anything. Their eyes are big and they're looking "over there, by the shore." They race off in a cloud of sand. Grandma follows more slowly, treasure map in hand. Grandpa stays by the fire even though he wants to go with them so bad he can taste it. Better that he's not too much around when the "treasure" is discovered.

Lori and I watch. Their daddy is still off fishing somewhere. Grandma is having a control problem. Kids are running in all directions. She's reading the instructions, pointing out the sketch to them.

"What are 'paces'?" "Which way?" "Nicky, paces are bigger than that." "I see it! I see it!" "There's the gnarly tree!" "Over here! Over here!"

Grandma follows along, herding them together;

almost having to sit on them 'til the next direction is examined. Patience is not an attribute of the young. Grandma has a little inside knowledge on the deal. Then, too, she can see grandpa's footprints in the sand. The pile of oyster shells is discovered. The "small hill of sand" creates momentary confusion. "Which way is 'sou'ward' ?"

Nicky, who has been following Josh up to here, suddenly runs ahead pointing, "There's a little hill of sand!" Away they go again, scrambling to be first to reach the site. Poor grandma. There's no way she's going to keep up. Grandpa chuckles to himself over this - not so anyone could notice of course.

"There! There's the little bush!"

". . . marked by the broken oar with which I busted. . ." Grandma reads on.

"There! There's the busted oar - and the life jacket!"

Nicky is on his knees digging in the sand with both hands. Josh joins in. Grandpa can contain himself no longer and is right there watching over their shoulders. "Bones! Yuckk! Grandma! Look! There's BONES!" A look of reproach is cast toward grandpa who busies himself with something else.

"Do ya think, maybe, that's 'Ole' Jim'?" Nicky looks up at his grandma. The bones are only a momentary diversion. The TREASURE is close at hand!

"Somethin' is here! Look! Look!"

The box is raised from the depths (maybe a foot)

where it has rested for, lo, this past hour or so. The lock and hasp are fastened in such a manner that they do not impair the opening of the box at all. Pretty clever, that grandpa, if I say so myself.

You know what happens next. They spill the whole thing in the sand. Then they grab at it to put it all back. Fortunately, grandma's cool head prevails and the treasure is salvaged.

Amid shouts of "Mommy" and "Daddy" and "Look!" and "Grandpa" they rush to where we're standing. "Look! There's another note."

Momma reads this next note - aloud, of course:

The Treasure
Aaargh, Mateys! This here treasure is to be used by them as finds it for anything whatever they wants, even candy or ice cream or even things that mommys and daddies don't want them to have.

Heave to, me Heartys, and have a good time!

Signed: Peg Leg Pete, the Pirate! his mark "X" (in real blood).

Their mom looks at grandpa and, through somewhat clenched teeth, mutters, "Daddy!" Have you ever noticed? Grandpas get blamed for everything! No wonder some of them become pirates.

That was a high point of Josh and Nicky's vacation.

I hadn't realized it would go over that well - or for that long. It's been awhile now and that's still their "Pirate Treasure." Little friends who disbelieve are showed the real-honest-to-gosh pirate chest with the lock and the map and the notes "signed in blood" and everything.

Someday they'll figure it all out. Someday.

I don't know if "Peg Leg Pete" or anyone else is aware of it but the kids weren't the only ones who discovered treasure on that trip to Port Aransas. Would I do it again? I can close my eyes and see Nicky and Joshua, eyes shining, digging in the sand, "treasure" in both hands. And Nicky looked up and saw me and he said, "You can have some too, grandpa."

Would I do it again? What do you think?

Life is Not a Destination

WHADDYA KNOW?

EDUCATION is man's going forward from cocksure IGNORANCE to thoughtful UNCERTAINTY

My grandson Levi Charlebois made a startling announcement to me the other day. In the course of discussing the merits of his "Monster Car," (with a "400 motor") and its' ability to go through (imaginary) mud, he paused, looked up at me and said, "I know everything."

Levi is four years old. He wasn't indicating that it was I, grandpa, who knew but that he, Levi, "knew everything." Well waddya say to that? I guess I have lost my standing among traditional grandpas of the world who are deemed to "know everything."

After the surprise – and amusement – of his off-hand remark I had to pause in my thinking. It set me remembering years gone by. Always in life there is the eternal puzzle over who knows or doesn't know or thinks they know. I have a weakness for remembering quips and quotes and flip remarks that seem to say profound things that seem to say more than they really say. For example:

> **"He who knows and knows not that he knows, he is asleep, wake him.**
> **He who knows not and knows that he knows not, he is uneducated, teach him.**
> **He who knows not and knows not that he knows not, he is a fool, shun him.**
> **He who knows and knows that he knows, he is a leader, follow him."**

If you're like me you'll have to read that over two or three times to get the sense of it.

While serving a tour in Viet Nam we had an officer we felt was in the "knows not and knows not that he knows not" mold. He wasn't a bad ol' boy actually but sometimes he needed an instruction sheet to remind him who the enemy was and which way to go to get there.

He was a military academy graduate and a real goer with the paperwork though. He probably went on to a glorious career in the Pentagon somewhere. That was probably a mean thing to say, wasn't it? Well, that's the thought that came along.

At another station, in my younger years I was enrolled in a night school course in calculus, advanced mathematics. The Air Force had an "enrichment" program to encourage the troops to better educate themselves. The Air Force would pay part of the expense for a person who wanted to get a higher education. I had a counselor who believed I was qualified for advanced training as an Aeronautical Engineer. In this calculus course I was enrolled in I was able to plug the numbers into the formulas and get the correct answers. As a result I was passing the course with flying colors – but I had no idea what I was doing. I finally screwed up my courage and cornered the instructor. Ignoring the adage that states, "It's better to remain silent and be thought a fool – than to speak and remove all doubt." In a quiet and private corner of the room I confessed my ignorance to him. I'll never forget his answer. He put his hand on my shoulder and said, "Son." (You have to remember I was much younger then.) He said, "Son, the first indication that you're learning anything at all is when you realize how much you don't know." Surprised, I looked at him, stuck out my hand and said, "Shake hands with a genius."

He went on to explain that what I was learning now

was "basic," the fundamentals, the juggling of figures and that later it would all come together and make sense. I never got to see it come together though. At the time I was an Aircraft Commander on a B-47 jet bomber crew. That was about the time Russia's Mr. Kruschev was caught putting ballistic missiles in Cuba. President Kennedy and General LeMay felt they might need me and my combat crew for more important things. But that's a whole 'nother story. There was some humor there too. Maybe we can talk about that another time.

One of the good things about Levi's "knowing everything" is that he's not lacking in self-confidence. He's not shy or withdrawn or afraid to say or do almost anything. His momma and poppa are doing a good job raising him in spite of grandma and grandpa spoiling him every chance we get. He seems to be developing into an outgoing extrovert, an explorer of things unknown. But of course Levi already knows everything.

I have a plaque on my office wall that I felt I should put his name on. It'll be a part of his inheritance if I don't give it to him sooner. The plaque states: "Education is man's going forward from cocksure ignorance to thoughtful uncertainty." I just hope he doesn't skin his nose too badly finding that out.

♎

It's what you learn after you think you know it all that matters.

Unknown

"THE UGLY ONE"

One year - oh - it must have been twenty years ago - the family was gathering for Thanksgiving. The kids ranged in age from eight into the teens. (I'm a grandpa - I can be "general" about that.)

One of the things we used to do back then - you might want to try this yourself - was to "hide" candy for the kids. We used those little silver-wrapped Hershey kisses.

Everybody knew what they were and they were easy for the kids to find. The "hiding" must be in plain sight, no turning things over or looking behind, and easily reached without climbing - even by the littlest ones. The number of candies hidden is important so you can say "three candies for each of you." When your three candies are found you have to stop to give the others an equal chance.

Since it was Thanksgiving their momma labeled the candies "Turkey Eggs." The kids were excited. Some of the older kids would "find" candies – would see them - but wouldn't let on so they could keep looking. We older folks were enjoying the scampering around, the excitement, the cries of joy when a child was successful. (Finding candy this way is not as easy as you might think - even though it's in plain view. Try it yourself.)

In the midst of all this merriment, a small voice from

someone who must have felt ignored was heard: "I'm ugly."

Ugly? Everything stopped! Everyone turned toward that small voice, the littlest one in the room. There was a rush to her side and many voices saying, " Oh, no, (I don't want to embarrass her after all these years by telling her name so I'll just call her "Mary.") Mary, you're not ugly!" (I'll bet you "Mary" will blush when she reads this.) Anyway everyone rushed to assure her that she was not ugly. Everyone that is - - except me.

"Yes she is," I said, "She's ugly as a mud fence." There was a sudden shocked silence, just for a moment, then everybody laughed - everybody but you-know-who. She looked at me with those big soft innocent eyes - and didn't know quite what to make of it.

She wasn't ugly! There's no such thing as an "ugly" little girl. Little boys - well - maybe when they're being mean, but little girls? Never! Everybody knew she wasn't ugly. And when everyone laughed at me, I think she knew she wasn't ugly either. All went back to searching for the "turkey eggs." It was a good Thanksgiving that year. Everyone had a good time and lots of good food - and candies - to eat. Ever after that, whenever I'd call on the phone or ask about her, I'd ask for "The Ugly One." Everyone knew about whom I was asking.

Many Thanksgivings have gone by since then. Sometimes we're together - sometimes not. The kids have grown, gotten married, are traveling their own paths. Thanksgivings aren't always together anymore but "turkey eggs" are still hidden by those kids for their children - or grandma and I for the grandchildren. It's still fun.

That little eight-year old "Ugly One" has grown into a beautiful young lady who's as pretty as she was when she was little. She went on to graduate from college, did an internship, and is now working at a job she enjoys, helping others, as a nutritionist at our local hospital. She married a really nice young fella' - I guess I'll just call him "Joe" - down Chatham way. They're both working at jobs they enjoy.

They have children of their own now, two little boys. We get to see them now and then - not as often as we'd like but that's life, isn't it? The little boys own their grandpa and I think they know it.

These days whenever I ask for "the ugly one," I always get a quick look and a warm smile. The turkey eggs are now for the grandchildren. The old style Thanksgivings seem to be fewer but the memories live on. Maybe, when the boys get bigger, those turkey eggs - and the story of "the ugly one" - will go on to create bright new memories for great grandchildren.

Ah, there's not much in this life quite like a happy smile of joy and excitement on a child's face. It's nice to see that smile when they're older too. Those are the things to be thankful for as we gather around a "turkey with all the fixin's" – and the kids hunt for turkey eggs.

If you're ever in a crowd, and think you know who "Mary" really is, just ask for "the ugly one." You'll recognize her right away. She may blush just a little but she'll also smile. You see, she'll be the prettiest girl in the room - pretty inside and out. Yes, she may be blushing but she'll be smiling too.

♎

"Beauty is altogether in the eye of the beholder"

General Lew Wallace

GRANDCHILDREN

This is a story about grandchildren. You younger folks better go study your schoolbooks or something. This may not interest you – at least not yet.

First the bad news – for me: there are times when I'm playing with and enjoying my grandchildren that a wave of guilt floods over me. I can't seem to remember doing these things with my own children.

Dorothy consoles me with several "outs" for these depressing moods. "Times were different then. Daddies had to work." "Husbands back then had to spend so much of their time just earning a living." "There were times when you . . ." That helps – a little – but you see I was a pilot, a flier and I really enjoyed flying airplanes Now I feel guilty about it. Was it right that I was enjoying life in the air instead of enjoying my children at home? Do any of you have similar feelings? Questions like that make for many hours spent staring deep into the fireplace. Aah but that's a whole 'nother story for another time and we won't go into that just now.

Now for the good news: if I had known grandchildren were so much fun I'd have had them first.

Little Hudson Charlebois is only two years old. When his momma brings him by for a visit he runs – runs mind you - to his grandpa with his arms stretched out to give grandpa a big hug. And that's about the bestest hug a grandpa can get. That little boy owns me – and I think he knows it.

There's a special place away back in the corner of the refrigerator where grandpa can find bits of chocolate now and then. That's when momma isn't looking of course - and Hudson knows that too. He's my boy.

Hudson has a brother – Levi. Levi is going on five years old now. You may remember my telling you a story or two ago that when he was just four years old, he informed me one day that he "knew everything." When Levi comes to visit he wants to go to the beach. Fortunately Hudson settles down for a nap just after lunch and I'm able to spend some time with Levi too.

Some days when Levi wants to go to the beach

grandpa's bones are telling him to stay close to the fire. You already know how that turns out. Grandpa ends up sitting on the beach in boots and hat and heavy shirt while Levi in his shorts plays in the waves. About the time I convince myself that a child's blood circulates faster than that of a normal adult a couple neighbors stroll by in shorts and halter-tops. "Isn't it a beautiful day?" they say. They're blithely taking in the sun. To heck with all of them! I start a little fire in the sand and sit close beside it.

Then Levi spots some tracks in the sand. It doesn't matter what made the tracks, to Levi they're "Tiger" tracks. Right away we have to find a couple of "guns" (driftwood sticks and a whole lot of imagination) and we go tiger hunting. He'll crawl in and out of brush piles you wouldn't believe. "C'mon grandpa." "Shhh!" "Watch now." "Be quiet." "I think he's over there." And we're off again.

We have a small "beach house" where our hunt will probably terminate. There's a cup of hot chocolate and a couple chocolate chip cookies stashed there. Then, if grandpa's lucky, it's back to grandma's house, back to tell grandma of our adventure. Surprisingly it's usually Levi's idea. Of course, as you can imagine, grandpa is sorely disappointed that we have to stop hunting tigers. Yeah he is. But Levi says, "Follow me, grandpa," and we're off again, off through the bushes. That boy just wants to make his own trail. I wonder if that's a premonition of his future?

When we get to the house Levi is usually in the mood for a short nap. But, by this time, his little brother Hudson is up, bright eyed and ready to go. With a little luck, grandma gets him interested in a video movie and grandpa gets to take a break too. At this stage grandpa may take an interest in Hudson's movies himself. Some of those children's movies are more entertaining than a lot of what adult "prime time" offers.

Are there other things grandpa could be doing? Some that maybe he should be doing? instead of "huntin' tigers?" out on the beach? Sure there are. Is grandpa going to quit the hunting or stop watching "Baby Einstein and the barnyard (or whatever)" and do them? Not on your life. After all, we can't have tigers roaming around on the beach and my little tiger hunter will grow out of that season all too quickly. Of course with another one running to his grandpa with his arms open I suspect, God willing, I'm going to be hunting tigers on the shores of Lake Superior for a few more years.

♎︎

These next two entries are poems, written by me, about my grandsons. If poetry is not your thing or you're not at the "mature" age where you appreciate grandchildren why just pass these up.

I'm their grandpa and if I want to write a poem about my grandchildren – and publish it – that's what I'm gonna do!

MY LITTLE GRANDSON, HUDSON
by "his grandpa"

His Momma named him "Hudson."

His Daddy calls him "Hud."

Grandma and I would love him

even if his name was mud.

When they bring him 'round to see us

and he runs into my arms

Why there's nothin' up in Heaven

that comes close to that boy's charm

Sometimes he and I'll wrestle

and tussle on the floor

'til grandma comes to tell us

we can't do that any more

He points at things and talks to me

and I'm not sure what he said.

Then grandma comes and gets him,

says it's time to go to bed.

She puts him in his little cot

in a room away from us

And tells me not to pay no mind

even if he makes a fuss

But, 'specially if I hear him,

My little Grandson, Hudson

I gotta sneak in there and spy

Cause he's wrapped around my heartstrings

and I hate to hear him cry.

But soon he's quiet and sleepin.'

I peep in from the door.

His grandma was right all along

as grandmas usually are.

Sometime he'll sleep a long long time,

sometime not long at all.

But his grandpa'll be there waitin'

outside the doorway, in the hall.

Then he's up, grandma changes his diaper,

puts "Baby Einstein" on TV.

While he watches the movie,

we're watchin' him, grandma and me.

'Til his momma comes to pick him up

then it's a hug and a wave bye bye

I gotta remember he'll soon be back

l'est a tear cloud up my eye

Yes, his momma named him Hudson

and his Dad may call him Hud

But Grandma and I want to share that boy

Anytime or place we could.

Here's the second poem - another grandson. I hope you enjoy it but I realize that poetry is a "hard sell." If you don't like it, well, you don't.

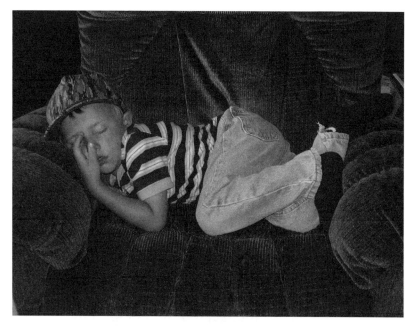

"LEVI"
by "his grandpa"

A little ray of sunshine came to our house today.

His momma brought him over,

said he could stay and play.

His grandma's there to meet him

as he walks up to the door

She greets him with a big warm hug,

his feet clean off the floor.

And he knows to take his shoes off

and he does it in a minute

And the house is never brighter

than when little Levi's in it.

Levi's daddy drives a tractor

and big trucks down on the farm.

So Levi's toys are tractors

and big trucks. It makes you warm

inside to watch him

makin' the engine roar

and his grandma's down there with him

drivin' tractors on the floor.

Grandpa watches, drinkin' coffee,

'til Levi calls, "I'm stuck."

Now it's grandpa's turn to join

and pull him out with another "truck"

He pulls him out – or pushes –

and then Levi's off again

"Levi"

And he wears grandpa and grandma out

just keepin' up with him.

Grandma starts a movie

about tractors on TV

And Levi stops to watch

and gives a break to her and me.

While he's watchin' his movie

I slip away for other chores

When it's over he'll be after us

to play with him once more.

Grandma seems to think it's naptime

but Levi doesn't agree

And he comes lookin' for Grandpa

and he knows where I'll be

He takes me by my finger

and looks up into my eyes

And there's nothing grandpa owns

he wouldn't give that little guy

'nen he leads me to the closet

and we both crowd inside

and we close the door and sit there.

It's a good place to hide

in case grandma wants to find us

but we don't really mind

'cause grandma's in the kitchen

makin' goodies for us to find.

Levi opens the closet door

and turns and tells me "stay."

Then he closes up the door again

and I hear him walk away.

He's after milk and cookies

grandma's fixed him on the table

And grandpa sneaks back out

to steal a cookie if he's able.

Then Levi grabs my finger again

and pulls me toward the door

And whatever I was doin's

not important anymore.

N'nen he pulls me clean outside,

"Levi"

holding his little hand

And he leads me to the sandbox

and we play there in the sand.

Or maybe he'll climb on Grandma's bed,

maybe jump up and down

Or crawl in on his belly

and pull the pillows 'round

and he'll lie real quiet

so no one knows he's there

and his grandma and his grandpa

they'll just "look" everywhere

"Where's Levi gone?" asks grandma.

"He's gone home," grandpa said

'nen Levi giggles and wiggles

so hard he shakes the bed

'nen grandma reaches under the pillow

and grabs him by the toe

and he squeals and throws the pillows off

and grandma lets him go

Sometimes he'll ride on grandpa's shoulders

and we'll walk down to the beach

and there's cookies in the beach house

and he knows right where to reach

to open up the cupboard

an the cookie jar he'll find.

Once he's chewin' on a cookie

it's the beach that's on his mind.

If I don't get his shoes off

he'll sure 'nuff get 'em wet

I look careful up and down the beach,

no one else is out there yet

So we don't just take the shoes off

but shirt and pants and more

And soon Levi's "skinny dippin',"

racin' waves that come ashore

He's hollerin' and squealin'

and splashing waves with glee

then he wants to build a castle –

"Levi"

and we do, Levi and me

We play 'til time to go back home

cause momma's on the way

and we don't want her angry

or he can't come another day.

And his momma comes to pick him up

and take him home again

And it's kind of sad to see him go

but he'll be back again.

And grandma and I wave goodbye

but we'll be countin' every minute

Cause our life is never brighter

than when little Levi's in it.

Life is Not a Destination

A BIG, WIDE, WONDERFUL WORLD

I had occasion to speak to a group of elementary school students the other day. "Elementary School" - you know - those are the kids who have the vague idea that maybe they're in school to learn something. They've not yet reached teenage where they suddenly realize that they know everything and, as dumb as adults seem to be, how in heck have we survived for so long?

We – I mean you older folks and I - can look back at where we've been, what we've done and maybe a few things we haven't done. From our vantage point down life's road we recognize some of the things that have

261

happened. Some things happened because of what we might do and some things happen in spite of us. So much has changed; so many things have been invented, so many things have been discovered, so many things have been created in our lifetimes.

To the younger generation – that is anyone who, when you mention Glenn Miller, says, "Who was that?" - the way it is today is the way it's always been. New things are happening faster these days. Instead of progressing in a sedate and linear manner – you know, 1,2,3,4 and so on – it advances geometrically, 2,4,8,16, thirty – whatever comes next.

It used to be we in Upper Michigan lived kind of on the outskirts of everything. We had to build, fix, repair and make do on our own. Today's world seems so complicated. Everything requires a specialist. The old family doctor used to come to the house with his little black bag and he treated and cured anything and everything. In the old days, between you and your neighbors, you could repair the plumbing, free sticking doors, level settling foundations and tune the family car. Tools required were a hammer, a pair of pliers, a screwdriver, some haywire and a whole lot of imagination. A rap on the side of the box would "tune" the old family radio. Things have changed.

Our horizons have expanded. That was something I tried to impress on those elementary school kids. It's hard for them to comprehend the need for abstract thoughts like "The square of the hypotenuse of a right triangle is equal to the sum of the squares of the other two sides." But all this apparently useless information is the foundation, the "launch pad' from which their lives can reach the stars. If you think elementary students aren't getting that level of education yet, look at how much farther they still have to go. But, like the rocket of that metaphor, if they don't get guidance both at home and in school, their trajectory may wander out of control. Their lives might tumble through space, hit or miss just as with an out-of-control rocket. Some may even self-destruct. That would be such a terrible waste.

So, how do you succeed in life? I told them that too. (You may have noticed that I'm a very modest fella.) I told them success was not measured by how much money a person had. I have known some wealthy people along life's path and more than half of them were not what I would call happy. Many were like the rest of us, kind of neutral. Their lives too experienced hills and valleys. And some of those wealthy individuals were seriously in need of psychiatric help. Success is doing the thing you enjoy doing and making a living at it.

The world will reward each of us in accordance with three criteria: What a person does, how well they do it, and how difficult it is to find someone else who can do it as well. Do the thing you enjoy doing. It's a cumulative thing. If a person enjoys what they do they'll do it well. They'll be curious about it. They'll learn more and more about it and do it better and better. The better they get the more successful they will be. Other people are inclined to call this "luck." The harder a person works the luckier they are and the greater the world will reward them.

Don't aim at a million dollars, just aim at being happy. Let the million dollars take care of itself. Then again a million dollars may carry so much responsibility it becomes a liability.

Here are the stages of education: first is a thirst for knowledge – the young kids. Next is the realization you already know everything – the teenagers. Third, and this is where you begin to come out of the woods, is when your attitude changes from knowing everything to not being sure of anything. That's when you realize how much you don't know. When an instructor I had told me that, I stuck out my hand and said, "Shake hands with a genius!"

The future of our nation - and the world – will be in the hands of those children. It's scary what they don't yet know but it's wondrous and exciting the many things they have to choose from.

I'd like to be able to do it again.

℧

"People who don't have dreams...don't have much."

unknown

Life is Not a Destination

Additional copies of this or any other of the author's books may be purchased through:

Still Waters Publishing
257 Lakewood Lane
Marquette, MI 49855-9508

(906) 249 9831

www.benmukkala.com
bmukk@chartermi.net

at the following prices:

"Thoughts Along the Way"	$ 15.95
"Life is Not a Destination"	$ 14.95
"Touring Guide; Big Bay & Huron Mountains	$ 9.95
"Come On Along"	$14.95
"Copper, Timber, Iron and Heart"	$15.95
Please add for shipping and handling	$ 5.00

Enjoy!

Ben Mukkala

Life is Not a Destination

Author

Ben Mukkala

is a native of Marquette, Michigan where he graduated from Gravaraet High School and Ball State University in Indiana. He enlisted in the U. S. Air Force during the Korean War, rose through the ranks, served a tour in Southeast Asia flying F-4 "Phantom" jet fighter-bombers. Ben retired in 1970 with the rank of Major.

After retirement, Ben flew various aircraft, sailed boats, and traveled. He enjoys the outdoors and an active life. He began writing during his Air Force career and been published in several flying and outdoor magazines and various newspapers. He has published several books.

He is the father of three daughters and one son, and stepfather to two sons and four daughters. He currently lives with his wife, Dorothy, in Marquette, Michigan.

"Sixty years ago I knew everything;

Now I know nothing.

Education is a progressive discovery

of our own ignorance."

Will Durant

"The mass of men lead lives

of quiet desperation"

Henry David Thoreau 1817 - 1862